Cat Calls

Janice Anderson

GUINNESS PUBLISHING

Acknowledgements

The author and publisher wish to thank the Random Century Group for permission to publish extracts from *Enthusiasms* by Bernard Levin (Jonathan Cape, 1983), and Alan Coren for permission to publish his 'And Moreover . . .' column which was first published in *The Times*, 7 December 1990.

Picture Credits

Suzanne Alexander (drawing page 55); British Museum; The Billie Love Historical Collection; Bruce Coleman Limited; Cambridge Newspapers Limited; Country Life; E.T. Archive; Explorer Archives; Hulton-Deutsch Collection; Mary Evans Picture Library; Spectrum Colour Library/Anne Cumbers; Times Newspapers Limited
Cartoons by Rob Heesom

Editor: Honor Head
Design and Layout: Michael Morey
Picture Editor: P. Alexander Goldberg

Copyright © Janice Anderson 1991
Publication copyright © Guinness Publishing Ltd 1991

Published in Great Britain by Guinness Publishing Ltd,
33 London Road, Enfield, Middlesex

Typeset in Itek Meridien by
Ace Filmsetting Ltd, Frome, Somerset
Printed and bound in Great Britain by
The Bath Press, Bath

'Guinness' is a registered trade mark of Guinness Publishing Ltd

A catalogue record for this book is available from the British Library

Contents

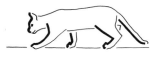

Cat Breeds 5

Part of the Family 29

Cat Care 49

Cats and Society 65

Cats' Tales 87

Cats' Skills 111

Cat Breeds

anx, or Tailless cat   Persian cat   Siamese cats
British wild cat   English cat – the biggest in the show   French African cat

The first important study of the physical nature of the cat was made by a distinguished Victorian veterinary surgeon, Sir George Mivart. In his massive book *The Cat: an Introduction to the Study of Backboned Animals*, Mivart wrote of the cat that 'its organization, considered absolutely in itself, is one of singular perfection and the adaption of means to ends which it displays is truly admirable'.

Since Sir George's book was published in 1881, the outward form of the cat has developed variations in colour, shape and form which would astonish any Victorian brought back into the world today. True, many of these 'variations' actually existed in Victorian times and have merely been introduced to the West from elsewhere, like the Turkish Van, the Singapura and the Korat. But it is still noteworthy that of today's more than one hundred recognized breeds and varieties of pedigree cat, many owe their outward form to the cleverness of the mating programmes devised by breeders or to the skill of cat lovers in preserving chance mutations thrown up by nature.

What Man has not changed is the basic animal beneath the fur, pedigree or moggie, the cat's organization of muscle and bone, tissue, nerve and cell, remains that which impressed Sir George Mivart deeply enough to lead him to write at the end of his book 'No more complete example of a perfectly organized being can well be found than that supplied by a member of what has no inconsiderable claims to be regarded as the highest mammalian family - the family Felidae.'

Variations On A Theme

There are 36 species of wild cat among the world's Felidae and only one domestic species, *Felis catus*, a species so well adapted to co-existing with human society that it far outnumbers all the world's wild cat species put together.

Felis catus is thought to have descended from two wild cats: the African wild cat (*Felis silvestris libyca*), plus something of the Asiatic desert cat (*Felis silvestris ornata*).

Although there are about 50 'basic' breeds of *Felis catus* recognized by cat fanciers today, with another 50 or so colour sub-forms recognized as separate breeds, there are not the marked differences in form between one cat and another that can be found among dogs. Dogs, having been bred for many purposes and to fulfil a wide variety of functions in human society, can show breeds like the St

The handsome Maine Coon is America's largest breed with a thick coat, large paws, long whiskers and 'a tail like a feather boa'.

Bernard and the Irish Wolf Hound at one end of the size scale and the Chihuahua and various other toy dogs at the other. Cats, whose

main function, apart from simply being part of the family, has been to catch mice and other vermin, can typically show a size difference between one breed and another of only a few pounds. True, there have been exceptionally large domestic cats – the size record was held for many years by a cat from Queensland, Australia, called Himmy who tipped the scales at 21.3 kg (46 lb) before his death – but on the whole, cats are like humans – much of a muchness.

Adult male moggies, fed sensible diets and leading reasonably active lives, weigh on average 4–4.5 kg (9–10 lb), with females being rather lighter than this. Among pedigree breeds, America's impressively beautiful Maine Coon can reach 13.5 kg (30 lb), but averages about 9 kg (20 lb), with a thick coat, a tail like a feather boa and paws 5 cm (2 in) across.

The Maine Coon, like the almost as big Norwegian Forest Cat, developed in a cold, northerly climate, where size is an important factor in survival. The world's smallest pedigree breed, the Singapura, sometimes called the 'drain cat', comes from the much hotter, steamy climate of Singapore and, though of a type familiar throughout Asia, is still rare in the United States, where it was imported as recently as the mid-1970s, and even rarer in Britain where the first Singapura arrived in 1989. Its smooth grace and pretty elegance should ensure its popularity as a house cat, as should its neat size: males weigh in at about 2.7 kg (6 lb) and females at about 1.75 kg (4 lb).

The Singapura is one of the latest in a long line of cat breeds originating in the Near or Far East, where cats have long been revered as sacred animals in many societies. In contrast, perhaps because cats held such a low status in the medieval Christian West and were the subject of appalling persecution, very few breeds can be said to have originated in Europe. There is the Norwegian Forest Cat, mentioned above, a breed so old as to have been the subject of Scandinavian folk tales; two shorthairs, the British and the French (the Chartreux); the tailless cat from the Isle of Man, the Manx which is said by some to have arrived there from a ship of the Spanish Armada which foundered in 1588; and, stretching a geographical point, the Russian Blue.

From the East, on the other hand, comes a centuries-old parade of feline beauty, from the Persian and Angora, out of 16th-century Iran and Turkey, to the Singapura and Korat, and taking in such widely loved breeds as the Siamese and Burmese from south-east Asia and the Egyptian Mau and the Abyssinian, both from North Africa.

The Newest Breeds

Nature, handing out genetic mutations with a not particularly liberal hand, has been responsible for the creation of numerous breeds of *Felis catus* around the world. Other breeds, first appearing as chance mutations in apparently ordinary litters, have been nurtured into long-term survival by breeders; the Cornish and Devon Rex cats are examples. But the largest proportion of the more than 100 breeds and varieties recognized in the world today have been the work of cat-loving humans, and many of them have been developed very recently indeed.

Here, as an indication of the sort of beauties Nature and cat lovers can create together, is a selection – in alphabetical order so as not to show favouritism – of the new pedigree breeds of our generation.

The **American Curl** is a cat with unusual ears. The first known American Curl was a stray which turned up in California in 1981. She was hard to miss, sitting there with her ears curving backwards over her head, and with hairy tufts growing out of the bases of those extraordinary ears. She produced kittens with the same curled-back, tufted ears and the gene for curled ears has proved to be dominant, allowing breeders to give the cat world a remarkable new breed.

The **American Wirehair** is a 1960s example of breeding from a mutant strain. This time, the queen involved was a shorthair from a farm in New York State who gave birth to a red-and-white male kitten with an amazing wavy coat, in which the guard hairs were bent and had hooked ends; the kitten also had crimped whiskers. That one kitten was to prove the basis of a new breed, which can be

This strikingly marked Egyptian Mau is a result of breeding programmes carried out with the specific aim of producing cats similar to the cats of Ancient Egypt.

outcrossed with the American Shorthair, so it is a healthy one, and can be produced in all the array of colours and coat patterns of the American Shorthair. The amount of 'wiring' in the coat can differ from cat to cat, some of them having coats which look quite normal but which are very dense and plush. The fur on a strongly 'wired' coat can become 'unwired', the hooks catching on a comb and getting pulled out, so it does not do to comb them too often. The American Wirehair is still relatively rare outside the USA, although breeding lines have been established in Canada and Germany.

The **Bengal** is another spectacular shorthaired cat from America, created by breeders in search of the exotic. The result of crossing a tabby cat with the Asian Leopard Cat, the Bengal really does look like something out of the jungles of Asia, as its thick, silky coat has dark spots on a 'rufus' ground colour. Its great, round eyes dominate its short-nosed face. All in all, a very attractive cat, and among the most expensive in the world, since there are still very few Bengals available.

The charming snub-nosed **Bicolour Longhair** has been in a class of its own only since the late 1960s. It must have only two colours – white plus any other solid colour – which should be evenly distributed over the cat's body in large, solid patches, with the white covering a maximum of half the cat, though it can cover as little as a third. Black-and-white was, perhaps not surprisingly, the original Bicolour form, and today black-and-white, cream-and-white, blue-and-white and red-and-white are among the most widely recognized varieties.

The glorious, green-eyed **Burmilla** has a precisely documented origin: an unplanned mating in 1981 between a Lilac Burmese queen and a Chinchilla stud, which produced four kittens. As is the only proper outcome of such a love match, the Burmilla is a lovely-looking cat, its short, dense coat being tipped, or shaded. The main ground colour is silver (or golden in a recent variety), tipped with

Two exquisite Cameo Longhair kittens. The combination of red and white tipping in their fur gives their coats a lovely shot-silk effect.

any one of the Burmese or standard colours. Its tail should be ringed in the same colour as the tipping. Bred from the same love match, the **Burmoire** has a coat that looks like watered silk – hence its name. It is a 'smoked' cat, with fur that is dark on top with silver colouring underneath.

The copper-eyed **Cameo Longhair** has been established since the 1950s. Breeders in the United States first produced it by mating smoke and tortoiseshell longhairs and now some nine varieties are recognized. They all have white undercoats, and the guard hairs, which are tipped to various lengths, can be cream, red, tabby or tortie coloured. The amount of tipping on the guard hairs decides whether the Red or Cream Cameo is a Shell variety (short tips), Shaded (longer tips), or Smoke (tips so long that the white undercoat can only be seen when the cat moves).

The **Cymric** was recognized as a breed in the 1980s, having been developed from mutant kittens found in Manx litters in the 1960s. Although its name is Welsh for 'Welsh', it is not known to have had any particular connections with Wales. The Cymric is a tailless cat, like the Manx, and comes in most of the recognized Manx colours, though its coat is medium-long and heavy.

The **Ocicat** is a spectacular shorthaired cat from America. It is a slim cat, elegant and graceful, as befits a felid with Siamese in its ancestry. The cat was developed by breeders trying to produce a Siamese with the markings of an Abyssinian; what they got was something that looked not unlike a little ocelot, hence it name. Its Abyssinian ancestry shows in the markings on its fine, glossy coat, which is ticked with several colour bands, the dark spots showing up well against a lighter background colour.

The **Ragdoll**, like many other new developments in society, came out of California in the 1960s. Although it was recognized as a breed in the United States in 1965, it is still relatively rare, though fast increasing in popularity outside America. It gets its name from the fact that, to a more marked degree than in other cats, it will flop in a totally relaxed manner over the arms of anyone picking it up – provided it is in the mood (if not, it will wriggle as firmly as any other cat). The Ragdoll is thought by many to have a higher tolerance to pain than other cats because, it is said, the first Ragdolls were born to a longhaired queen, possibly an Angora, which had been hurt in a road accident. This seems to be a misconception, and Ragdoll owners are adamant that their cats are normal in every respect; in 1988 the British Ragdoll Club went to the trouble of having two Ragdolls officially examined by a leading scientist at the Glasgow Veterinary School, who pronounced them 'normal members of the cat family'.

Normal, but not ordinary. Ragdolls are, in fact, very beautiful longhairs, with markedly affectionate natures. They are large cats – up to 7–9 kg (15–20 lb) in adult males – which will take 3–4 years to reach full size. Coat shadings and point colours also take up to three years to develop fully. Three coat patterns are presently recognized: Bi-Colour, Colourpoint and Mitted (which means that the cat has white mittens on its front paws, matching a white chest, bib and chain).

The **Rex**, so named because its coat reminded its original breeders of their Rex rabbits, is another cat with crinkly short hair. In fact, there are two English Rexes, for the **Devon Rex** has been proved to be the result of a quite different genetic mutation from the **Cornish Rex**. The latter first turned up as a cream, wavy-haired male, called Kallibunker, in a litter of farm cats in Cornwall in 1950. When mated back to its mother, it bred true. When a similar kitten appeared in a Devon litter in the early 1960s, it was crossed with a cat of the Cornish type, but the result was straight-haired kittens. Since then the two Rexes have been developed separately.

They are both very affectionate cats, more strongly drawn to people than to territory. Both have a foreign appearance, being slender, even skinny little cats, with long, slim legs. Both have wedge-shaped heads, with large ears, though the Devon Rex's face

This Devon Rex kitten's head looks too delicate to support those enormous ears! As the kitten grows older, its very short suede-like coat will become rather more dense.

Three charming Cornish Rex cats, showing the short, plushy coats and crinkled whiskers for which the breed is famous. The Rex's coat may curl, wave or ripple, especially on its back and tail.

is not as long as the Cornish Rex's and its very big ears, set low on the head, give it an elfin look.

The Rex's coat is very short and close-lying, with no guard hairs. The Cornish Rex's fur is rather more silky than that of the Devon Rex, whose coat can contain a few guard hairs. Although records show crinkly-haired kittens turning up in Europe and America around the mid-1940s, it was the appearance of the two English versions which gave an impetus to their development and there are now American and German Rexes being bred. They come in a wide range of colours and coat patterns, and there is even a 'Siamese' variety, called the Si-Rex, which has the conformation of the Rex with Siamese points markings.

The 1960s proved to be an interesting decade for cat breeders, for another positive mutation of the time was the **Scottish Fold**, a shorthaired cat with folded-forward ears which first appeared in a farm cat's litter in 1961. The gene for folded ears proved positive and the cat has been bred successfully since, though it is more popular in Europe and the USA than in Britain. Some people believe that the folded-over ears could tend to impair the cat's hearing and may also lead to ear parasites and infections. Not so, say other breeders, and point to the Scottish Fold's gentle nature, placid temperament and pleasantly round and chubby face as excellent reasons for having it in the family.

The **Somali** is another breed that was developed in the United States in the 1960s. Essentially, Somalis are longhaired versions of the Abyssinian, which many people believe is descended from the cats of Ancient Egypt. Both cats have a 'ticked' coat, though the Somali's has many more bands of colour on the hairs of its coat, which gives it a splendidly rich density of colour, whether it is the Usual or Ruddy variety (the latter is golden-brown, ticked with darker brown or black), the Sorrel (or Red – copper ticked with chocolate), or the recently recognized Silver Sorrel (sorrel top coat and pale underneath). The Somali also seems to have inherited its Abyssinian ancestor's temperament which, though friendly and good-tempered, needs to be allowed to work off its energies outside the house. Not the ideal cat for a city flat!

A beautiful example of the Somali, showing the dense, fine-haired coat for which this breed is noted.

'A skin like a peach' is the way admirers of the rare Sphynx describe the hairless cat's body. Originally known as the Canadian Hairless, the Sphynx was bred in Canada.

From the sublime to the . . . well, not ridiculous, perhaps, but certainly rather strange, is the **Sphynx**, because its hair is so short as to have virtually disappeared. Hairless cats have been known in history, but the last, the Mexican Hairless, is thought to have died out around the turn of the century. The Sphynx turned up as a mutant kitten, quite hairless, in a litter born to an ordinary black-and-white cat in Canada in 1966. The kitten was saved and later mated with its mother to found the breed, originally called the Canadian Hairless. The Sphynx is still very rare, even in North America; there are few breeders and the Sphynx produces smaller litters than average, so there may never be many of them around. In 1990 there were estimated to be fewer than 40 in the world. Even so, £4000-plus, which was the asking price from breeders in the late 1980s, seems a bit steep . . .

The golden-eyed **Tiffany** has nothing to do with smart New York jewellery stores. It is, in fact, a longhaired version of that elegant, shorthaired cat from south-east Asia, the Burmese, and was developed in America by cat fanciers who crossed Burmese cats with Longhairs. In the United States only the original sable brown variety is recognized, and in Britain breeders are hoping for recognition of this and other varieties.

The **Tonkinese** is another shorthaired American creation, the product of mating Siamese and Burmese cats. Although some Tonkinese cats were produced in the USA in the 1930s, when they were called Golden Siamese, the breed was not developed in a big way until the 1960s, by which time it had been renamed 'Tonkinese'. They are very slim and elegant cats, as befits their ancestry, and are said to be very affectionate, with a great capacity for liking people – some owners say they are just downright nosy!

Although the Tonkinese has been fully recognized by cat associations in America since the 1980s, it has not yet achieved anything like universal recognition, largely because it does not breed true: a Tonkinese pair can produce Siamese, Burmese or Tonkinese kittens. In Britain, only one cat association recognizes the Tonkinese, though the Red Point variety is a British production which, with its beautiful colour, like a Red Burmese with darker Siamese-type points, should do a lot to attract attention – and recognition.

The **Turkish Van** cat is not a new breed, but is one that is new to the West, having been discovered by two British cat lovers, brought home and successfully bred from. The Turkish Van hails from remote Lake Van, in south-eastern Turkey, where it was domesticated several hundred years ago. Perhaps because it lived near water for so long, it loves playing around in water, which is why it was soon dubbed the Swimming Cat in the West. Its markings are distinctive and uniquely beautiful: auburn markings (or delicate cream in a new variety) on the face and tail, which stand out against the overall chalky-white of the Van's long, silky fur. (As is not surprising in a cat from a country with marked extremes of climate, the Van moults heavily in the summer and may even look like a shorthaired cat, but come the winter and its coat is long and heavy again.)

There is always a white patch on the Van's forehead, between the auburn markings around the ears, which Turkish people will tell you is the mark of Allah. Not that many Turkish Van cats encountered in the West today will be all that close to Muslim Turkey: the first examples of the breed were imported into Britain in the 1950s and breed recognition was granted in 1969. It has also been growing in popularity in Australia and the USA in recent years.

With cat fanciers so devoted to producing cats of ever more individual coats and colours, and to creating pets perfectly suited to modern life, there are sure to be more new breeds appearing – like the **mini-Himalayans** recently reported as having been created by a New York pet store especially for keeping in small apartments. Called **Colourpoints** in the UK, Himalayans are longhaired cats with Siamese coat patterns, and the New York pet store's versions were guaranteed not to grow bigger than a four-month-old kitten, which they achieved by mating the runts of litters over several generations.

Nor should it be forgotten that Nature will undoubtedly have more surprises up her sleeve, some of which could lead to new breeds. To keep a sense of proportion, however, here is the story of a strange genetic mutation that did not make it to breed status.

In this instance, the birth of the peculiar-looking female kitten took place in the US state of North Carolina in 1936. The queen was an ordinary pet cat who, it was reported, had been involved in fights with a mongrel dog before her kittens were born, and had been badly frightened by the dog on several occasions.

The freak kitten, called Nonesuch, had the face of a black, white and yellow spotted dog; its ears were quite long and sharp-pointed; it had the short whiskers of a puppy, its hind legs were bowed and its tail was stubby. Even more odd was the fact that this kitten had the short, smooth hair of a dog all over its body. It came into the world about 12 hours after the rest of the litter, with its eyes open and able to crawl a little. Surely, asked Mr Henry Sternberger, when reporting this kitten's birth to the *American Journal of Heredity*, the only plausible explanation for all this was those frightening dog fights experienced by the mother cat before her kittens were born?

Not so, thought the *Journal*'s editor, geneticists would be more inclined to ascribe the unusual animal to a genetic mutation. Still, the *Journal of Heredity* was sufficiently interested in the story of Nonesuch to report in September 1937 that the cat, when six weeks or so short of her first birthday, had given birth to a litter of four perfectly normal kittens. She herself continued to look more like a dog than a cat, with head, ears and shoulders like a fox terrier, and with many doglike actions.

Colour Points

The most obvious difference between one cat and another is colour.
Size of body and length of coat both lose significance for the eye
confronted by a blaze of red, a glistening array of stripes, or the
gleaming shine of a smooth black coat.

The main colours which combined to make up the myriad shadings of today's cats, both pedigree and moggie, all have histories
which are interesting – and colourful!

Black Cats

Despite having been around for such a long time, pure black cats
are relatively rare. It is very hard to produce a cat whose black coat
is completely free of white hairs or, if it is a longhair, of a smoky
shadowing. And many otherwise totally black cats have a white
'locket' under their chin. Too much sun can bleach out black, leaving black shorthairs who like sunbathing with a distint brownish
hue to their coats and giving longhairs a slightly bleached-out look.

More than any other colour, black has associations of luck, both
good and bad, attached to it. In **Britain**, there is an old saying in
northern parts that goes, 'Wherever the cat of the house is black, the
lasses of lovers will have no lack', and it is believed that for a black
cat to walk across the path of a newly wedded couple is an indication of good luck and happiness ahead. In contrast, in the **United
States**, black cats are considered to bring bad luck: 'it is bad luck to
see a black cat before breakfast', they say in the mid-west states, and
'when you see a black cat, turn round seven times, or you will have
bad luck', they believe in other parts of the States.

In France, also, many people believe that black cats can mean
bad luck. In Brittany there is an old tale, still told, that on every
black cat is one white hair and if you can find it and pull it out
without being scratched by the cat, you will have won a unique
good luck charm which could help make you rich or lucky in love.

The belief that black brings good luck could well be an inversion
of the medieval Christian belief in witches and the role of the black
cat as the Devil's servant: if no harm came to you as the result of a

black cat walking across your path, then you had been lucky indeed.

The blackest cat of all, for most cat lovers, is the gleaming satin-black **Bombay**. This is a fairly recent, man-made breed, created in the United States by mating an American Black Shorthair and a brown Burmese. The result was the superb Bombay, with the look of a little black panther and a coat like patent leather.

There have been many famous black cats. **Charles I**, England's martyr king, had a favourite black cat which went everywhere with him because he believed the cat was his luck. 'My luck is gone', he is said to have cried as he mourned the cat's death.

Ludovic the Cruel was a black Angora belonging to **Cardinal Richelieu**, ruler of France in all but name in the 17th century and a famous cat lover; Ludovic is said to have slept peacefully on his master's lap while the Cardinal signed death warrants for the enemies of the French state.

Taki, the black Persian pet of the writer **Raymond Chandler**,

The lighter side of a grim man: Cardinal Richelieu neglecting affairs of state to play with his cats. So devoted was the Cardinal to his pampered pets that he left pensions for 14 of them in his will – a fact not passed on to Swiss Mercenary guards at Versailles who massacred most of Richelieu's cats shortly after his death.

This is 13-year-old Blackie, displaying the relaxed attitude of a cat who knows he is in the money. In 1991, Blackie inherited £50,000 in the will of his owner, Mrs Muriel Fletcher. Ready to keep Blackie in his accustomed style are Don and Mimi Cottrell, at whose cattery in Brixham, Devon, Blackie took his holidays while Mrs Fletcher went on her annual cruise. Now Blackie is permanently part of the Cottrell family.

featured on the covers of his master's books in the 1940s and '50s.

Peter was the name of a succession of black cats employed by the **Home Office** in London. The last one was a black Manx which, because it was a female, had its name subtly changed to **Peta**.

Clementine was a black moggie famous for spending much of its time sleeping among the organ pipes in St Clement Dane's church in London.

Pussy was an ordinary family pet who achieved extraordinary fame in 1988 when it was revealed that her owner, **Mrs Dorothy Walker**, had bequeathed £2.7 million to the Royal Society for the Prevention of Cruelty to Animals on condition that the charity look after Pussy for the rest of her life.

Finally, a grand salute for **Dirty Dick**, a superb Black Longhair, who was 14 times overall cat show grand champion in the United States in the early 1900s.

Tabby Cats

The tabby pattern – dark markings, spots or stripes on a paler background – is the oldest known in the domestic cat and, because the tabby gene is a dominant one, is also the most common colour form. It turns up, albeit rather paler in tone than today's tabby, in Egyptian wall paintings 3,000–4,000 years old, confirmation of the theory that our domestic cat is descended from the African wild cat, which the Ancient Egyptians are thought to have domesticated. The stronger tabby marking is thought to have developed when the original Egyptian cat, spread round the Mediterranean world by traders such as the Phoenicians, met and mated with the sturdy European wild cat.

The earliest tabbies were striped – the now quite rare pattern called 'mackerel'; it is thought that the classic blotched tabby pattern first appeared in Britain in the reign of Elizabeth I. To settle any arguments, tabbies have dark stripes on a pale background, not the other way round.

The 'Spottie' – the **British Spotted Shorthair** – is essentially a **Mackerel Tabby** in which the markings are broken up into spots.

In a pedigree cat, the spot colour should match the coat colour. Today's 'Spottie' is very like the cat of Ancient Egypt which had a prominent place in Egyptian mythology as the destroyer of the Serpent of Evil.

The tabby is a very bejewelled cat. Many tabby cats have 'rings' on their tails and 'bracelets' on their legs, and they display 'necklace' stripes across their chest. Pedigree Classic varieties of tabby, whether short- or longhaired, should have a butterfly shape on the shoulders, from which three stripes run down the spine to the tail, and an oyster-shaped spiral on each flank. And, of course, no tabby worth the name is complete without that most characteristic tabby marking on the forehead: the 'M' worn like a pendant between the ears.

Why 'tabby'? The name derives from the name of an area in the old city of **Baghdad**, **Attabiya**, in which watered silk, known in Europe as tabby silk, was first made. The wavy pattern in the silk's weave suggested the pattern of markings on the tabby cat.

'In the dark, all cats are grey,' says the old proverb. In fact, night or day, there is no such thing as a grey tabby. Look hard at the hairs of a tabby's coat, and you will see that they are banded with black, brown and yellow, a colouring called '**agouti**'. The grey is an optical illusion created by the merging of the colours.

Blotched tabbies were the ships' cats of the British Empire, with examples of the breed being taken all over the world in British ships from the time of the Elizabethan voyagers on, and they proved dominant enough to flourish wherever they went ashore. One writer has gone so far as to dub them 'the British Imperial Cat'. It is, therefore, only historically right and proper that the world's heaviest cat, **Himmy**, mentioned earlier in this chapter, should have been a tabby from **Australia**, and that the 'most prolific mother' record should be held by another tabby: **Dusty**, from **Texas**, with 420 kittens to her credit.

Selima, 'demurest of the tabby kind', who drowned in a tub of goldfishes, and was immortalised in Thomas Gray's *Ode*, really existed. She was the favourite cat of the 18th-century writer **Horace Walpole**.

White Cats

White cats were the first longhaired cats to appear in Europe. These were Angoras introduced from the Middle East in the 16th century, and their fur was very fine. Today's White Longhair is a Victorian creation, developed by mating Angoras with coarser-haired white Persians. The pedigree British White Shorthair is also a late Victorian development.

This is not to say that white cats have not been around for some time, for they have been known for centuries. They can be found in large groupings on the edges of **Europe** – in Scotland, on the Isle of Man and on the isolated Faroe Islands and in Iceland. A leading American cat geneticist, Dr Neil Todd, sees the hand of man in this. He believes that those great explorers and voyagers, the Vikings, took their white cats with them in their longships, as well as taking them overland on journeys as far from home as Turkey: hence, the beautiful white cats with auburn markings found around Lake Van in southern Turkey.

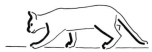

Both shorthaired and longhaired white cats with blue eyes are prone to deafness because of a side effect of the gene which gives the cats their white colour. Cats with other coloured eyes may also be affected. Odd-eyed cats – one eye orange, the other blue – may be deaf on their blue-eyed side.

'**Silver**' cats get their colour from black tipping on white fur. In perfect Chinchilla Longhairs, the white fur must be snow white, to which the black tipping gives a sparkling effect. The variety of Chinchilla called the Shaded Silver Longhair has a heavier tipping, so that the basic white colour is overshadowed by silver on the cat's face, sides and tail.

By the time you get to 'Smoke' in the breed catalogues, you are well away from the delicate tipping of the Chinchilla, for the smoke colour is achieved by a deep tipping – that is, the black or blue extends a long way down the hair, right up to the roots in Britain and leaving white roots in American breeds. The undercoat is white or silver, which produces a shimmering effect when the cat moves, and the light colour shows through the dark.

Cats specially named for their white feet include the **Snowshoes**, nicknamed 'Silver Laces', which was bred in America specifically to combine Siamese-type points with the white feet of the Birman, and the **Mitted Ragdoll**, which has white mitten and boots. In cat breeding parlance, 'gloves' are smaller than 'gauntlets' and slightly smaller than 'mitts'. The Birman has 'gloves' on its front paws.

Owners of white cats have to take particular care of them in the summer, because of the delicate pink skin under their fur. Just as the skins of very fair people can react badly to too much sun, so can that of white cats. If you encounter a white cat with white cream on his ear tips, it is probably a sign of a caring owner, who has used zinc and castor oil ointment, or a cream from the vet, to protect the exposed ear tips from too much sun.

White Angoras were the great love of **Mde du Deffand**, an 18th-century woman of letters. She offered two of them to her fellow cat lover, the English writer Horace Walpole, but the letters of neither tell us whether the cats ever made the journey from France to England.

A famous white longhair of our day was **Solomon**, a Chinchilla, who advertised carpets with languorous grace on television and then went on to movie fame as the villain's pet cat in the James Bond movie, *Diamonds Are Forever*.

A white New York stray, found in an alley in a Christmas-time snowstorm, has now become the hero of two best-selling books. **Cleveland Amory**, founder of The Fund for Animals, an anti-cruelty organization with its headquarters in New York, found the cat and told his story, including how he came to be named **Polar Bear**, in *The Cat Who Came For Christmas*. Now Polar Bear and the self-styled curmudgeonly Mr Amory have continued the story of their life together in *The Cat and The Curmudgeon*.

Tortoiseshell Cats

Tortoiseshell cats have a coat which is mottled red (ginger) and black. When white or cream is present as well, the effect is to patch the coat with large areas of red, black and white (or cream). To British eyes, the effect is rather like that of the shell of a tortoise, hence the name. Americans think the patched tortoiseshell and white pattern looks like printed cotton, hence their name, **Calico**, for these cats. Tortoiseshell and white shorthairs were once called **Chintz**, so fabric seems uppermost in everyone's minds when looking at these pretty cats. In one of the new varieties of tortoiseshell and white shorthairs, blue and cream have been introduced to the coat in place of black and red, producing a very appealing pale cat.

Because the genes which carry the tortoiseshell colouring are sex-linked, most tortoiseshells are female. The chances of a male kitten turning up in a tortoiseshell litter, because of some genetic mishap, are estimated at about 200 to 1. Any male kitten that is born is virtually certain to be sterile. All in all, the breeding of tortoiseshell kittens is a difficult business.

In many parts of the world tortoiseshell cats are thought to be lucky. In **Britain**, it was once believed that stroking warts with the tip of a tortoiseshell's tail could cause them to disappear, the remedy being most effective during May (thus setting up a conflict of belief with that other widely held view that May kittens bring snakes into the house and, if allowed to grow up, are bad, troublesome cats). In the Celtic parts of Britain, tortoiseshell cats have long been welcomed in the house, in the belief that they will bring good health to the family, views similar to those held in many parts of the **United States**, where Calico cats are said to bring good luck.

In the **Far East**, tortoiseshell cats are traditionally ideal to have on board ship, where their chief function is to frighten off storm devils.

Because they are so pretty, tortoiseshell cats have been used as models by numerous artists. **Gwen John**'s drawings and paintings of her cats have proved very popular this century, both in the sale room and as reproductions on prints and cards. One of her favourite models was her lovely tortoiseshell who, although a female, was called **Edgar Quinet**, after the Paris street in which Gwen John lived, which was itself named after a celebrated French writer and extreme left-wing politician.

Edgar Allan Poe may have set a black cat at the heart of one of his most chilling stories, but his own beloved pet was a large and good-natured tortoiseshell called **Catarina**.

Ginger Cats

'Ginger', 'marmalade', 'orange', 'flame' and 'yellow' are all popular names for the colour known to pedigree cat breeders as 'red'. Ginger cats so pale as to be a beige colour are called 'cream' by breeders. As with the tortoiseshell colouring, the gene which produces ginger is sex-linked, but this time maleness predominates and most, but not all, ginger cats are male. That there are more ginger females than tortoiseshell males born is due to the fact that matings between ginger or cream toms and ginger, cream or tortoiseshell queens may well result in female ginger kittens. Such kittens are also more likely to grow up fertile than male tortoiseshells.

Ginger cats, although known in Britain for centuries, are less common than blacks or tabbies, even though they are themselves basically tabbies: hence their stripes. There is, however, a high concentration of ginger cats in North Africa and, animal geneticists have noted, a marked distribution of ginger cats along a route from the Mediterranean to London. This trail corresponds with an ancient trade route across Europe from North Africa, suggesting that ginger cats either followed the traders or were an item of trade themselves.

Ginger cats generally have equable, calm natures, which makes them popular with animal trainers and anyone professionally involved with animal photography, such as film and television advertisement makers. Some of the most famous film-world cats have been ginger, including the **American** cat **Morris**, perhaps the most famous of all feline stars, who won a PATSY (Picture Animal Top Star of the Year) award for the splendid way in which he promoted a brand of cat food on American television for many years. The cat which featured in the films *Rhubarb* and *Breakfast at Tiffanys* was also ginger.

There have been numerous real-life ginger cats to have achieved fame, too. Not the least of them was **Sir Winston Churchill**'s beloved **Jock**. There is still a ginger cat in residence at Chartwell, Sir Winston's house in Kent, kept there by the National Trust in compliance with Sir Winston's will, which directed that a marmalade cat should always be 'in comfortable residence' at Chartwell. He left a sum of money to cover the cat's costs, so the National Trust is not out of pocket over the matter.

Mis, a ginger cat from **Denmark**, achieved fame – or, perhaps, notoriety – by being named the fattest cat in Europe. Since he weighed in at 15 kg (33 lb) in his heyday, there could not have been many contenders for his title.

Blue Cats

The 'blue' colour in such breeds as the British and Russian Blues, the French Chartreux and the Blue Longhair is really grey – a dilute form of black. It is the result of the black pigmentation in the coat hairs being diluted. The colour blue is not a new one for cats; it was known in France in the Middle Ages, where the Chartreux is said to have been developed by the monks of the famous monastery of La Grande Chartreuse, in Renaissance Italy, and in Russia, from where Russian Blues, then known as Archangel cats, were taken to Elizabethan England.

Wide-eyed innocence displayed by two Blue Burmese kittens. The first Blue Burmese turned up in 1955, in a British litter bred from an imported American father. Within five years, enough blue-to-blue matings had taken place to produce pure-bred kittens and the Blue Burmese was given breed status.

Blue Longhairs, known in Europe for several centuries, became very popular in Britain in the late 19th century. Even Queen Victoria was a fan, owning two prize-winning blue Persians. The Blue Persian Society was founded in 1901, just too late to have Queen Victoria as its first patron.

Blue is a colour confined very largely to pedigree cats, since the gene for the dilute colouring is recessive: the gene which influences the denser colourings of your average moggie is a dominant one.

Perhaps the most famous of all blue cats is the Russian Blue which belonged to **Czar Nicholas I** of **Russia**. Called **Vashka**, this pampered animal is said to have lived off best Russian caviar (Beluga, no doubt) poached in champagne and other delicacies. Russian Blues are an omen of good luck in Russia, but even so there cannot have been many who have lived the life of Vashka.

The silver-blue, green-eyed **Korat**, one of the world's oldest cat breeds, comes from the same part of south-east Asia as the Siamese. Both cats are included in the famous 14th-century Siamese book, *Cat Book Poems*, now in the Thailand National Library in Bangkok. The book's description of the Korat is beautiful in its evocation of nature: 'The hairs are smooth, with tips like clouds and roots like silver. The eyes shine like dewdrops on a lotus leaf.' Rare even in Thailand, the Korat is even rarer in Britain and the USA though it is recognized as a breed by the cat fancy in both countries.

Part Of The Family

A drawing from an Ancient Egyptian papyrus in the British Museum, showing the sun god, Ra, in the form of a cat, slaying the serpent of darkness, Apep. The Egyptians believed the battle between the two was eternal, taking place in the underworld when the sun disappeared below the horizon every night.

The date by which cats stopped being wild and began to live in houses with humans is not known, though it can be guessed at. Some historians and archaeologists put it as quite late Egyptian, only a few centuries before the Romans, while others point to finds which could date the domestication of the cat to a much earlier period, around 6000 BC, approximately 2000 years later than the dog is thought to have been domesticated.

The famous Egyptian *Book of the Dead*, thought to date from before the First Dynasty, refers to the cat as a symbol of Ra, the Sun-God, whose myth is related in the Book. The British Museum's papyrus copy of *The Book of the Dead* has a picture of the god Ra in cat form, with a knife in one forepaw and the head of a huge python, symbol of Ra's rival Apep, held firmly under the other.

As recently as 1983, a French archaeologist, Alain le Brun, found a feline jawbone while excavating a Neolithic settlement, dated at 6000 BC, on the island of Cyprus. Cyprus is known not to have had an indigenous wild cat population, so the cat whose jawbone was left on the Neolithic site was not a wild cat and must have been brought to the island from the mainland of the Eastern Mediterranean, presumably by the people who established the settlement.

It is possible that at that time the cat was not in people's living places, but it could well have been in their granaries and food stores, guarding them from mice and other vermin and at the same time providing itself with shelter, food and a safe place for its kittens, all within sight and sound of Man.

Some 4000 years later, the cat was certainly well entrenched in Egyptian society and in its religion. At Bubastis, centre of the worship of the great Cat-Goddess Bast (or Pasht), sacred cats were tended by priests in Bast's sanctuary. At Beni-Hassan, on the Nile 250 km (160 miles) above Cairo, a temple was dedicated to Bast in 1500 BC; over the years thousands of mummified cats were sent to the temple from all over Egypt for careful burial. A few of these cats are now in museums, the only survivors of the destruction of the burial site in the 19th century, when 300,000 mummified cats were dug up, shipped to England and sold as fertilizer.

To us, it seems an extraordinarily insensitive way to have treated the burial site and is, perhaps, a sign that cats, although long-established as household pets, had not quite recovered the place in European society they had held before the great persecutions endured by them for several centuries in the medieval Christian West.

Cats would seem to have been well treated by the Romans, who apparently preferred polecats and weasels to cats as mouse catchers, valuing the cat more for its fur. In the post-Roman world, including Britain to which cats were probably brought by Phoenician traders, the Romans and the Vikings, cats were still well regarded.

In 808 the Emperor Charlemagne had to regulate the sale of otter and cat furs, so fashionable had they become in the wardrobes of the rich; by the next century, it was the cat's vermin-catching skills that were earning it its place in society, not its fur. A code of laws from 10th-century south-east Wales included a picturesquely suitable fine for the crime of killing or stealing a cat that guarded the King's house or barn: '[the cat] is to be held with its head to the ground and its tail up . . . and then clean wheat is to be poured about it, until the tip of the tail be hidden; and that is its worth'.

A few centuries later began that period of persecution throughout Europe, with the cat seen as the Devil's creature, a familiar of witches and a focus of black magic.

As late as the 17th century, Edward Topsell, writing a serious description of the beasts of his age, could say of the cat, 'It is needless to spend any time about her loving nature to man, how she flattereth by rubbing her skinne against one's legges . . .' and then go on to note that '. . . the familiars of Witches do most ordinarily appear in the shape of Cattes, which is an argument that this Beaste is dangerous to soule and bodie'.

Just a generation later, Samuel Pepys recorded in his diary the careful way in which a cat was rescued alive from the Great Fire of London and Sir Isaac Newton, as well as becoming the greatest scientist of his age, could find time to invent the precursor of the cat flap for the convenience of his own cats.

By one of those ironies of history, at about the same time as the last trial for witchcraft was taking place in the New World in 1867 – when the 'proof' of the witchcraft included that old accusation of associating with cats – in Europe the new Age of the Cat was dawning.

The first book to study seriously the history and background of the cat in Britain, C. H. Ross's *The Book of Cats*, was published in 1868 and was followed two years later in France by Champfleury's *Le Chat*. In the 1870s the great Crystal Palace cat shows were established, giving a boost to the cat fancy, and popular interest in the cat grew apace.

Today, the cat has penetrated every part of our society and there are few aspects of the way we live which do not take the cat into account in some way.

New Arrivals

Kittens are very special little animals. The writer Saki made the general point well: 'Confront a child, a puppy and a kitten with sudden danger; the child will turn instinctively for assistance, the puppy will grovel in abject submission, the kitten will brace its tiny body for a frantic resistance.'

To move from the general to the particular: on 6 September 1950, a four-month-old kitten followed a party of climbers right to the 4,548-metre (14,780-foot) summit of the Matterhorn.

These strong-willed little creatures come into most people's lives as adorable, wide-eyed balls of fur aged, at their youngest, nine weeks or so. How they come into the world and grow up is fascinating in itself . . .

Birth Minus 63 Days Or So

A cat's pregnancy lasts 63 days on average, though litters may be born at anything from 56 to 70 days after conception. Longer pregnancies are more likely in queens living comfortable indoor lives than in outdoor cats. Very premature kittens, born before the 56th day or so, do not often survive. So, owners who know their queen has mated, can count forward nine weeks on the calendar and mark with a big red X the day by which everything should be ready for the kittens' appearance. If the mating date is not known, but suspected, owners should look out for signs of the queen 'pinking up' – her nipples turning pink and becoming rather swollen about 2½–3 weeks after she has mated – and estimate 6 weeks from this as the likely birth day.

What To Expect

In the 1970s two queens, one in South Africa and one in the United States, each produced huge, record-breaking litters of 14 kittens, though five of the American Calicoes were born dead. These are still the largest domestic cat litters recorded, but to get things in perspective: according to statisticians, the mean litter size of the domestic cat is about 3.8 kittens. The ideal sized litter is said to be 3 or 4 kittens; too many more and the mother cat may not be able to cope on her own, especially if it is her first litter.

Tom cats may go on siring offspring until they are 16, and female cats have produced kittens at 12 (the equivalent to the mid-60s in human females), though with older cats the litter is likely to be small, often only one kitten. Even so, over the years a female cat can give birth to literally hundreds of kittens. The record is held by a tabby from Texas called Dusty, who produced 420.

Pedigree cats, lacking the rude hybrid vigour of moggies, do not usually breed for so long.

As for colour and even hair length, surprises could be in store, for not only may the queen and tom be carrying genes for colours other than those they display themselves, but it is also possible for the queen to have mated with several toms and be carrying kittens fathered by all or any of them, depending on which tom's sperm fertilized which of her eggs. (This multi-fathering of a litter is called 'superfecundation'.)

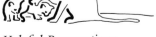

Helpful Preparations

Like all expectant mothers, a pregnant cat needs a good, well-balanced diet, and her usual brand of cat food may not have sufficient vitamins and minerals. Vets, to whom the queen should have been taken for an ante-natal checkup (which should include the administering of a pregnancy-safe worming drug to ensure the kittens are not born with worms), can supply vitamins and mineral supplements in several forms.

While the queen should be given every opportunity to choose and prepare her nest herself well before her kittens are due, a special kittening box prepared by her owners in a quiet, warm place is likely to be more convenient for everyone. Few queens living in family houses are likely to go to the lengths of the famous cat in Argentina who produced three litters in the six years she chose to live up a tree in Buenos Aires, but do you really want a handful of kittens born in your laundry basket or airing cupboard or on the family sofa?

It is a good idea to keep the queen indoors during what should be the last two weeks of her pregnancy. It will be easier to notice if anything is going wrong or when she is clearly close to giving birth, when she will be restless, perhaps calling at times, and will not want to eat a few hours before she goes into labour.

Birth Day

Kittens are normally born head first, or tail first with their hind legs extended. They manage the difficult business of taking their first breath by themselves, before their umbilical cord is severed by their mother and the placenta dispelled (usually to be eaten by the mother; it is actually a good source of extra nourishment for her). The mother stimulates her kitten's breathing and circulation when she licks him clean after his birth. A kitten's average birth weight is around 100g (4oz).

The newborn kitten cannot see or hear because his eyes and ears are tightly closed, but he has good senses of smell and touch (much of the latter through his vibrissae or whiskers). He cannot walk or crawl, but can move around the nest, because he must be able to find a teat – his mother is not going to put him on one. He moves by pushing with his hind legs and 'paddling' with his front legs. He can move his head from side to side. The newborn kitten's instinct to find a teat and begin suckling is very strong, and he is usually attached to a teat 30 minutes or so after his birth.

Within 24 hours of his birth, the kitten will spit or hiss at anything unusual, like a strong smell or being handled by people.

A kitten around a week old . . . his eyes are already open but his movements are minimal.

At Seven Days

By now the kitten will have doubled in weight and will have been feeding from his own preferred teat for several days. He will have learnt to 'knead' his mother to stimulate the flow of milk.

His eyes may be starting to open, though they may not do so for another 10 or 12 days. They will be pale blue and probably only capable of seeing patches of light and shade and shadowy movements. He will be starting to hear sounds, too.

The last of the umbilical cord is usually lost by the end of the kitten's first week of life.

At Two To Three Weeks

The kitten will be starting to crawl, albeit in a very unsure and wobbly way. At three weeks he will be four times his birth weight and thus have better control of his muscles.

At this time, his milk teeth will start to show, incisors first, then the canines. His molars will not appear until he is about six months old and getting his permanent teeth.

He will look alert now, with open eyes and pricked ears. Up till now his mother has helped him to urinate and defecate by licking his genital region to stimulate the right actions. Three weeks after birth is about the right time for him to be introduced to a litter tray – one big enough for him and his brothers and sisters to play about in – and to put him into it every time he looks as if he might be wanting to use it for its proper purpose.

At Four To Five Weeks

The kitten is now at an equivalent stage to an 18-month-old child. He is ready to leave the warm family nest, to tumble about and play with toys, hooking them towards him with his front paws. He should also have started washing and grooming himself by this age.

Weaning can begin around four weeks, with the kitten being given powdered cat milk substitute, or perhaps unsweetened evaporated milk. Many kittens enjoy baby cereal or puréed baby food.

Between Seven And Eight Weeks

Still growing rapidly, the kitten will be taking part in pretend fights with his peers, going 'hunting' and showing great curiosity in everything about him. He will be showing increasing independence, deciding for himself when he wants to eat and sleep, and where.

Most kittens are fully weaned at eight weeks, and capable of living independent lives – as long as there are humans about to provide food and such comforts as a clean litter tray (he is still too young and small to cope with a cat flap).

By eight weeks, all his milk teeth should have appeared.

Nine Weeks

This is the time to give kittens their first vaccinations against Feline Influenza and Feline Infective Enteritis, two potentially lethal infections of the upper respiratory region. A second vaccination should be given about three to four weeks after the first, with booster shots annually thereafter.

At Twelve Weeks

Another month older, and now the kitten's eyes are changing from blue to their adult colouring. From about now his permanent teeth will begin to push through.

His mother will have stopped letting him suckle by now, and may even be fiercely rejecting any advances. This is because she could be ready to mate and start the pregnancy and birth cycle all over again. In any event, a kitten will be completely independent of his mother by the age of six months, when he is himself a young cat. If kittens are not to be bred from, they should be neutered. Female kittens can be spayed at 16 weeks and tom kittens castrated at 36 weeks. Both operations are simple, safe and painless, and highly desirable in a world where the lives of unwanted kittens can be cruel and very short. There is no need to worry about the species becoming extinct; the Cat Protection League recently estimated that one unneutered female could produce about 20,000 descendants in five years.

Choosing A Kitten

Pedigree kittens may be obtained, for a price, from reputable breeders. Samples of recent Pedigree prices are: British Blue, £50–£250; Burmese, £100–£150; Maine Coone, £400; Persian, £150–£400; and Siamese, £75–£150. 'Pet quality' kittens will cost less than 'show quality'.

Moggies may be found through friends, from the litters of neighbours' cats, or from cat homes and animal rescue centres. It is not wise to buy a kitten from a pet shop, since there is no guarantee that the kitten has not been in contact with animals harbouring diseases or infections, or that it has been fed properly while in the shop; nor will the buyer, in most cases, be able to discover anything of the kitten's parentage or background.

When choosing from a litter, many people will be attracted first by colour; maybe they loved the Orlando stories as a child, so they will go for the marmalade kitten; or perhaps they have always had a tabby in the house, so will choose another one.

More important than colour are the particular points which should be noted about any kitten:

Is the fur in good condition? It should be smooth and sleek with no bare patches and no scabs on the skin beneath. Part the hairs and look for any signs of parasites, such as fleas, which may show up themselves, but are more likely to have left the small black specks which are tell-tale signs of their presence.

Do the eyes and ears look good? The eyes should look clear and bright, with no discharge in the corners and no sign of the 'haw' (the 'third eyelid', or nictitating membrane). The ears should also be free of dirt or discharge.

The nose pad should be cool and slightly moist (a warm pad is usually a sign of fever), and the nostrils should be clean and definitely not runny.

Is the kitten clean and dry under its tail? A dirty bottom could indicate diarrhoea and scalded areas urinary problems. An educated look under the tail will also tell you if the kitten is male or female. This may not be important in the long run, as most caring owners have their kittens neutered.

Try to have a look in its mouth. It should have the right number of teeth for its age, they should be clean and set straight in clean pink gums.

Finally, and most important of all, is the kitten alert and lively? A healthy litter and a healthy mother will all look active and interested in their surroundings – and in you.

A point to keep in mind: cats generally plan their families for the summer months, so this is when kittens are far more likely to be available. In mid-winter, 1991, a nationwide shortage of kittens was reported in the United Kingdom, with suppliers unable to keep up with the enormous demand. One Sunday newspaper also noted that responsible bodies like the Cat Protection League put prospective kitten or cat owners through vetting procedures 'scarcely less rigorous than those of child adoption agencies'. While prospective owners might be vetting cats on the lines suggested above, they could themselves be checked out for the following: would they promise to have their cat neutered; would they keep the cat in at night, safe from cat poachers and speeding cars; were their homes well placed for cats to grow up in safely and in comfort; would they themselves be at home during the day to provide the cat with necessary companionship; and, finally, were they sure they could afford the expense, including food and veterinary care, of a cat about the house?

There was good reason behind the insistence that owners should promise to have their new cats neutered: despite 'seasonal' shortages, the RSPCA still has to 'humanely destroy' 12,000 unwanted newborn kittens and puppies in Britain every year.

Swiss-born cat artist Théophile Steinlen captures perfectly some of the attitudes regularly adopted by cats eager for food. The cats in this picture were probably Steinlen's own; his house in Paris, known as Cats' Corner, sheltered large numbers of strays, many of whom appeared in his posters and drawings.

Food For Thought

Somewhere in California a businessman is doing sell selling mineral water in bottles specially labelled to appeal to cats and dogs, on the grounds that if he does not care to drink the water that comes out of his kitchen tap, why should it be foisted on his family pets? Meanwhile in Japan, Ajinomoto General Foods has launched a cat food low in magnesium and rich in vitamin E, specially to help prevent heart disease, and Nippon Pet Food has produced for cats

Vita-One Mix, scientifically researched and formulated, for 'ease of digestion'.

What the Californian and the Japanese have in common is an awareness that cat food is big business – really big, multi-billion-dollar business.

In the United States, where the figure for cat food sales exceeded that for baby food at the end of the 1980s, about $2 billion-worth of prepared foods goes into cat bowls and saucers every year.

In Britain, where over four-and-a-half million households contain 6.9 million cats, £429 million is spent every year on canned cat food, and another £3.8 million on biscuits and 'treats' for cats. (These are 1989 figures, the latest available at the time of writing.)

In the European Community, nearly one in two of its 96 million households keep at least one pet, with 17.1 per cent of them owning a cat. There are estimated to be 25 million pet cats in the European Community, including Britain. For them, the European pet food industry produces 980,000 tonnes of canned foods every year and another 179,000 tonnes of other kinds of food. Turnover value of all this in 1986, the latest year for which figures are available was 3,188,000,000 ecus.

The advantage to owners of feeding their cats out of cans from reputable manufacturers is that they know the contents have been specially formulated to provide a balanced diet. Cats are not as easy to feed on fresh food as dogs because the detailed requirements of their diet are quite complex. Unlike dogs, cats are natural carnivores who need to eat foods high in good quality animal protein to provide the right amounts of the special amino acids their bodies require, which they cannot make themselves. A lack of the amino acid taurine can lead to progressive retinal atrophy and, over a period, to blindness. Thus, it is very difficult to keep a cat healthy on a strictly vegetarian diet.

What Should Be On The Menu

The average-size adult cat requires an intake of 350 kilocalories every day to keep healthy, which is three times as many, weight for weight, as the average human adult. One 400g (14oz) can of cat food contains roughly this number, as does about 200g (7oz) of fresh fatty red meat.

Essential in the cat's diet is high-quality animal protein, which should make up at least a quarter of an adult cat's diet, and up to 40 per cent of a kitten's. If their protein does not come from canned food, then it can come from red meat, fish, poultry, eggs, cheese and milk. Fats are an important source of calories, especially for older cats. Minerals and vitamins are also important, but, on the whole, cats should not need supplements if they are getting a healthy, well-balanced diet. Like humans, cats need some filler foods to provide carbohydrates and fibre; bread, pasta and cereals are all good, as are fruit and vegetables. Water is essential, though cats do not necessarily have to lap it out of a saucer. Meat has a high water content, and a can of cat food has a moisture content of about 80 per cent; even so, fresh water should always be made available to a cat.

All the above could come from mice; your average house mouse contains about 15 per cent protein, plus 10 per cent fat, 70 per cent water, a little carbohydrate and vitamins, calcium and phosphorus. Since most house cats are content to kill mice and then lay them neatly out for their owners' admiration, mice cannot be considered a good basis for a well-balanced diet.

Cats should not be fed offal too often, because of its very high vitamin A content. Once or twice a week is enough for that liver the cat likes so much. Sorry, puss!

Fish for cats should always be cooked, though not boiled, since boiling destroys many nutrients. Raw fish contains an enzyme called thiaminase which destroys thiamine (vitamin B1).

Raw egg white is not good for cats, as it contains a chemical which neutralizes an important B vitamin. Raw yolk is fine. Two eggs a week are enough for cats.

Too much milk is not good for cats, either. Many cats are allergic to the lactose in cows' milk, which is also too strong for small kittens to digest. If a cat wants lots of milk, try offering it reconstituted dried milk or evaporated milk mixed with water, in proportions of about 1 to 2.

Cats eat grass because they know instinctively that the vitamins it contains are good for them, and because it is a natural emetic, helping the cat to regurgitate fur balls.

Cats have a weak taste response to sweet foods. It was once thought that they could not taste sweet foods at all, but numerous scientific experiments have nailed this myth. What has been proved is that the 'sweetness factor' is not important to a cat when it chooses what food to eat. In fact, cats do not have to taste food at all to know whether they are going to enjoy eating it; smelling it is enough. The cat's nose, responding strongly to the food's smell, tells them all they need to know. So there is no point in crying, 'You could at least try it!' after a cat who has sniffed at his food and walked off – he already has, with his nose.

For a cat, perfect food does not come straight from the refrigerator. He likes his food at the same temperature as his tongue – about 86°F.

Catnip, or catmint, is not a food, but a herb, *Nepeta cataria*, to which many cats respond with remarkable enthusiasm. It contains a chemical called nepetalactone which works on the cat's nervous system (when it is sniffed, not eaten). Cats which respond to it become relaxed and playful at the same time. It is used to stuff toy mice for cats to play with, and can be sprinkled on the food of a cat that has not been eating too enthusiastically. It is perfectly safe and is not addictive.

Reading The Label On The Can

All but five per cent of the pet food manufacturers in the UK belong to the Pet Food Manufacturers' Association and follow its guidelines, based on current government regulations, about what should and should not be in a can of cat food.

What, basically, is in the can is animal-based protein from 'those parts of the carcase that custom and usage dictate are unsuitable for human consumption', to quote the Association's information profile. Since 1989, the can will not have cattle brain or offal in it; nor will it contain any kangaroo, whale, pony or horse meat. The label on the can will not be much more specific, but it still pays to know the meaning behind the words.

First of all, canned cat foods should be described on their labels as being either 'complete' or 'complementary'. 'Complete' cat foods (which on US labels may be called 'complete', 'balanced' or 'scientific') must by law contain carefully balanced amounts of the nutrients, vitamins and minerals the cat needs for good health. 'Complementary' indicates the food is not a complete one and the cat may need supplements, which may be indicated on the label.

Labels may also describe the contents of the can as being 'rabbit flavour' or 'chicken flavour' – which means just that: the 'flavour' may be present in the can, but not necessarily the rabbit or chicken meat. If the can says 'rabbit flavoured', then the can must contain at least some rabbit meat. If the label says 'with rabbit', then there will certainly be some rabbit in the food, but there will also be lots of other meat. Only with the more expensive 'gourmet' cat foods can you be sure of getting a high proportion of the food named on the label, though the amount may vary from 25–100 per cent, depending on the brand.

The other item to look at carefully on the label is the small table of protein, ash and cereal amounts in the can. A protein content of 7½–8 per cent is fully adequate for the cat's needs; a low level of ash is also desirable, and very little cereal.

What Goes In Must Come Out

Figures released by the RSPCA in 1990 revealed that British dogs deposit 1000 tons of faeces on our green and pleasant land every day. Which is another reason for cat owners to feel smug: at least cats are pretty good at burying their waste matter. Helping them to be clean-living has also become big business. Americans buy a million tons of specially formulated cat litter for their pets every year and British sales of cat litter are soaring, having reached about £40 million in 1989/90.

Eatable Hazards

Many cats like nibbling houseplants and some like nothing better than nipping flowers out of vases and either chewing them or rearranging them on table or floor to suit their idea of the perfect flower arrangement. In either event, the cats' owners should know that a number of houseplants and garden flowers are toxic to cats and should be kept well out of their way, whether they are plant nibblers or not.

Among dangerous houseplants are philodendrons, the Dieffenbachia species, true ivies (Hederas), elephants' ears (Caladium species), poinsettias, false Jerusalem cherry (Solanum capiscastrum), castor oil plants and pot azaleas.

Out in the garden, many flowers and plants can make cats ill if they are eaten. Among the more common ones are azaleas and rhododendrons, the common laurel (Primus laurocherasus), mistletoe, broom, laburnum, chrysanthemums (which can be grown indoors as pot plants, too), crocuses, daffodils, hyacinths, lily-of-the-valley, larkspur, lupins and foxgloves.

Still in the garden, cat owners should remember their pets and read the labels carefully before they use weed-killers in the garden or on the lawn, slug pellets, creosote on the fence, paint, paraffin or turpentine, or other poisons and chemicals. Some can kill cats or at least make them quite ill. And cats do not have to eat them to be affected. They can breathe them in, absorb them through their skin and, obviously, lick them up while grooming themselves.

Another potential killer in the garden is the common toad, which carries in those warts on its back a virulent poison called bufotalin. Most cats, spurred into action by the sight of a toad hopping in its ungainly manner across the lawn, will sink their teeth into it and experience such an instant reaction to the poison that they will drop the toad and suffer nothing worse than a period of acute discomfort. Only a really persistent attack could result in the cat getting so much poison in its mouth that it suffers a major reaction.

Walkies!

Cats were once kept on leashes in Japan. We know because it is recorded that in 1602 the Kyoto government passed a law which

This is Sheba, a cat who thought that, in many respects, she was a dog. Giving the lie to the generally held belief that black cats won't be trained, Sheba went everywhere on a lead. When in her owners' car, she was kept on her lead, but allowed to sit on her own window shelf.

45

ordered cats to be released from their leashes. Three centuries later in Edwardian England, we find a photograph of a cat show held outdoors in Richmond Park, in which all the cats entered in a longhair class are shown sitting or standing at their ease, each one on the end of an elegant ribbon lead.

This would not happen today, partly because we have come to believe that it is not right for such independent creatures to be put on leads, and partly because most cats are not naturally as amenable as dogs to being taken for walks on a lead. They can be trained to like leads, though the training should start when the cats are young. Some breeds are more disposed to the business than others. Both the Tonkinese and Burmese can be trained to walk happily on a lead, and cat fanciers also suggest the Siamese, Rex, Maine Coon and Egyptian Mau (an Oriental Tabby type) as breeds which may be trained to enjoy going out for walks with their owners, provided training is started early.

The most suitable type of lead includes a harness, not just a collar round the cat's neck, which it could slip out of or choke on. An H-shaped harness, which buckles round the chest and neck, is generally recommended as the safest kind.

If your cat is a black one or an unneutered tom, don't even consider trying to get it used to a lead: they are both regarded as being almost impossible to train.

Pampered Pussies

Some people will go to great lengths to give their pets an idyllic existence. Pretentious Pets, a London-based company specializing in designer accessories, knows of a couple in Los Angeles who built a swimming pool alongside their own for their English bulldog; presumably, if they acquired a Turkish Van cat, they would build a third pool especially for it. Meanwhile, the company has narrowed its horizons for British cats, whose owners are, on the whole, less over-the-top in their ambitions for their pets. Individual horoscopes cast to order for their cats, or a special ceramic porringer shaped like a reclining feline are more the sort of thing British owners may request from the company.

To judge by the range of accessories currently available for British cats, eating and sleeping are the two areas of a cat's life of most concern to their doting owners.

Feeding accessories include the sensibly down-to-earth 48-hour timed feeder, available in several forms, and designed to serve meals to a cat left at home on its own. The feeder comes with an ice-pack to keep the food fresh and a battery to operate the door-opening timer. At the top end of the financial scale come items like the silver-plated feeding bowl, engraved with the cat's name, available at over £100 from a leading London jeweller and silversmith.

As for sleeping quarters for the well-housed British cat, these could range from mail order luxury blankets carefully constructed from non-absorbent, but machine washable, polyester fleece with a slip-resistant backing to a giant-size slipper made of blue denim with red plush lining. If slippers are not to a cat's liking, he could have his own padded fabric country cottage to slip into, a padded fabric medieval castle, or – better still, perhaps – a white plush bed, this time mouse-shaped with pink ears, whiskers and a tail.

For cats of discernment, to whom all this padded whimsy could seem a bit naff, a simple fur-fabric-covered radiator cradle, designed to fix over most central heating radiators, could provide many hours of blissful warmth. Cats with a sense of history might prefer a Georgian-style solid mahogany four-poster bed (£600, excluding bedding) or a Victorian-style pine bed (£140 or so), both of which are miniature reproductions made especially for pets. Cats whose tastes run to the trendily modern might prefer the bean

This climbing frame would make a delightful gift for any cat bored with chasing mice.

Most pussy cats will find this warm and cosy radiator cradle blissful so long as they don't suffer from vertigo!

bags filled with fire-resistant polystyrene beads which are a popular item in the brochures of a Midlands mail order company.

Out of bed and ready for some action, our pampered pussy can be kept amused at little cost with a range of toys from a nationwide supermarket chain, or it may be offered more elaborate toys like a carpet-covered pyramid with play ball attached, or a scratching post with ditto.

To go outside, the cat, wearing a magnet on its collar – probably fine leather carefully chosen in a colour to suit its fur and with its name imprinted on it – will push its way through the latest in electronic cat flaps, complete with see-through front and four-way manual lock and an electronic circuit, which allow the cat flap to open only to the cat with the magnet on its collar.

Should the pampered puss wish to go on a holiday of its own while its owners are abroad, then it does not have to make do with any old cattery, for there are now a number of five-star luxury animal hotels in Britain. At one in Cheshire, cats are offered a range of condominiums with names like the Royal Suite, the Safari Suite and the Kentucky Suite. Inside the suites are brass rocking cradle beds and balconies covered with fake grass; food is best-quality, thoroughly tested cat food, though it might be disguised on the menu, pinned outside the office every day, as Cat's Pyjamas, or some such. Meanwhile, over in Cambridgeshire, our pampered puss's cousin could be enjoying itself on a pets' health farm, where exclusive natural diets are on offer in the luxury of heated accommodation.

And there is no denying that some of the pampered pussies could need a health farm. British vets issue warnings time and again about the dangers of overfeeding, which can make cats not just obese but susceptible to many internal problems such as blocked bowels or malfunctioning kidneys and to dental problems, too.

In the United States, a man called Steve Malarkey has made a video especially for cats. He scattered 91 kg (200 lb) of birdseed in his back garden, set up a video camera, and shot enough film of the birds and squirrels collecting and eating the seed to make a video 25 minutes long. He has called it *Catnap* and is marketing it in the States at the equivalent of £10.

Mr Malarkey is planning to launch the video in the UK, and expects the same enthusiastic response from British cats as he gets from American: 'Some sit transfixed, others press with their paws and scream . . . and some jump on the TV,' he reports.

Maybe Mr Malarkey should widen his horizons. How about *Cataerobics* or the *Good Catkeeping Diet*? Such videos might help keep the modern pampered pussy as healthy, or, at least, as exercise- and diet-conscious as its owners.

Cat Care

Cats live much longer now than they did even 30 or 40 years ago. In the 1950s, thousands of kittens died in their first few weeks of life because of cat flu and feline enteritis; today, vaccinations successfully control these epidemic diseases. Though thousands of cats are killed on our roads every year, many more can be saved than once was the case, so great have been the advances in the technology of veterinary medicine and surgery.

Researchers at the University of California's Davis School of Medicine used a robot surgeon to perform a hip replacement operation on a dog in 1990; the robot was the unusual thing, not the hip replacement, for animals, including cats, can now have hip replacements, pacemakers inserted, plastic surgery, corneal grafts and open-heart surgery, just like humans.

Perhaps most important of all in the long term, the manufacture of pet food has undergone a transformation, backed by the force of law and government regulations, so that the cans of 'complete' food for cats on the supermarket shelves provide them with a healthy, life-enhancing diet.

All of which means that when a new cat is brought into the home, it could well be there as part of the family for around 15 years, which is double the average age cats were expected to attain earlier this century. More than ever, it is every owner's responsibility to know enough about their cat's needs, in sickness and in health, to ensure that its life is as contented and happy as possible.

Grooming

Regular grooming is essential because it helps eliminate parasites like fleas, and also because it cuts down on the amount of hair cats ingest while cleaning themselves; fur balls can obstruct a cat's bowel and cause problems which may need surgery to put right. Longhaired cats need to be groomed at least once a day, using a bristle brush or a double comb (one with fine teeth on one side and heavier teeth on the other) and a grooming powder, such as fuller's earth or talcum powder. For shorthaired cats, once or twice a week is sufficient, again using a brush or comb, with perhaps a chamois leather or piece of silk to give the cat's fur a final 'polish'.

The grooming period is also a good time to check over the cat's ears, eyes, claws and teeth for any signs of trouble, and to look carefully in the fur and on the skin for any telltale signs of fleas and other parasites.

Everything to hand to groom a white longhaired cat, whose fur needs daily attention. Proprietary dry shampoos or, in the case of this cat, talcum powder, can be sprinkled on the coat and then brushed out, bringing dirt, dust and loose hairs with it.

Cats who spend all their lives indoors and never get near a tree or wooden fence to file their nails on, may need to have their claws trimmed. Special clippers are available to make it easier to do the job, which should involve just the very tip of the claw, and never further back along the claw where the quick grows. A cat's claws should never be removed in their entirety. Indeed, it is unlikely that a vet could be found in Britain who would perform such a needlessly cruel and painful operation.

Regular cleaning is important for the teeth, a practice which it is sensible to begin when the cat is young. Feeding has a part to play in teeth care, for eating raw meat occasionally or crunchy cat food regularly helps clean deposits of dirt off the teeth and prevent tartar forming. A cat's teeth may be cleaned with a soft child-size toothbrush – if the cat will let you: otherwise regular visits to the vet for descaling are a good idea.

If a cat needs to be bathed, it should be washed with a specially for-mulated cat shampoo, not detergent or the family shampoo from the bathroom which could severely irritate a cat's skin. Most cat care books will talk with some insouciance about bathing cats, as if it were an everyday thing in the cat world. The truth is, many cats find the whole thing deeply unpleasant and will fight against it with every claw and tooth at their disposal. Some experts suggest putting the cat up to his neck in a pillowcase with a dollop of cat shampoo, immersing it in a basin of warm water (using the elbow test, as with babies' baths, to ensure the temperature is all right), then massaging the shampoo into the cat's fur through the pillowcase. Rinsing the shampoo out again will take two or three changes of water in the basin.

An alternative way of cleaning a dirty cat is to give it a bran bath, which involves massaging bran warmed in the oven to a very warm but not too-hot-to-touch temperature into the cat's coat, wrapping the cat in a warm towel for a good ten minutes, then carefully brushing out the bran, a section of the coat at a time. Done thoroughly, this is a surprisingly effective way of cleaning a cat.

Grooming time is when external parasites, and even internal ones like worms, may come to light, so it is as well to know what to look out for and what to do about it.

Fleas have become an all-year-round parasite of the domestic cat living in centrally-heated, wall-to-wall carpeted houses – an en-vironment which suits fleas down to the ground. Cat fleas do not, on the whole, bother humans, though they can bite and they are unpleasant and unhygienic things to have about the house. They can seriously bother a cat, however, causing allergic reactions and eczema and they can be very debilitating, especially if a cat swal-lows infected fleas, when tapeworms are the all-too-likely result. Fleas should not be allowed to get out of hand. One flea can lay 300 or so eggs a month, of which the great majority will hatch. Multiply this by the number of fleas on the cat – it is never going to be just one – and, if left untreated, a major infestation could be the result.

Apart from the small reddish-brown fleas themselves, the most obvious sign of the presence of fleas on a cat is the black specks of their droppings in the fur. To check that the specks are flea drop-pings and not dust, comb them out of the cat, then put them on a piece of damp kitchen paper or tissue, where, if they are droppings, they will turn red as the blood they contain seeps out on to the paper.

While fleas can be caught in a comb, they then have to be killed quickly before they hop away, and combing is unlikely to be 100 per cent effective. Fleas can be controlled by using sprays or powders, obtainable from vets, chemist shops or pet shops. Many cats do not like being sprayed, because the hiss from the container sounds like an attacker, so they will need to be treated with a powder, which is more time-consuming. Beds and sleeping places should also be sprayed. Both sprays and powders must be used with great care, following pack instructions to the letter. Nor are most of them suitable for young kittens, and a vet's advice should always be sought before treating kittens with fleas.

The most common of the intestinal worms which can afflict cats in temperate climates are two varieties of roundworm and tapeworm. Roundworms lay eggs which are passed in the cat's faeces, while live tapeworm segments, looking like grains of rice, will show up round the cat's anus and in its bedding. Drugs will successfully eliminate both kinds of worm and dramatic improvements in a cat's condition, including his eating habits, will show quite quickly after the drugs have been administered. All kittens and cats should be wormed regularly, even if they are showing no symptoms of harbouring the parasites.

Other parasites a cat may pick up include lice, mites and ticks, which many anti-flea products will also kill off. Ticks should be dealt with by the vet, since pulling them off when the teeth are still buried in their host's skin can cause abscesses.

Ringworm is not an insect but a fungus which can form circular scaly bald patches on the cat's skin. Veterinary help is needed to get rid of it. An anti-fungal wash is usually sufficient for mild cases, but for severe cases special drugs may have to prescribed. Since ringworm can be passed from one cat to another, and also to humans, an infected cat should be quarantined from other cats while it is being treated and its sleeping places thoroughly disinfected. Bedding, toys and grooming equipment would all need to be burned.

First Aid

First aid is the help and care you can give an injured cat before it gets to the vet. It is not, except in minor cases, a replacement for the vet's professional help and care.

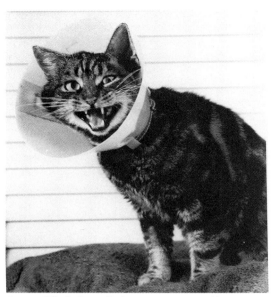

A paper 'Elizabethan collar' prevents a cat scratching or biting at skin infections or wounds, thus speeding the healing process.

Many of the items useful in tending a wounded or sick cat will already be in the bathroom cabinet or first aid box. Useful extras include liquid paraffin, petroleum jelly, hydrogen peroxide, a rectal thermometer (one with a blunt or rounded mercury bulb) and an antiseptic suitable for use on cats; Dettol is one such and so is saline solution (a teaspoon of salt in a pint of warm water), which is easily made up and very useful for cut paws. Antiseptics containing phenols, carbolic or coal tar are toxic to cats, which puts household names such as Savlon (liquid) and TCP out of bounds as far as the family pet is concerned.

Situations in which immediate first aid is essential can arise all too suddenly in a cat's life. Here we look at the most common:

Accidents A cat that has been hurt in an accident should be moved as little as possible and its head should not be raised. It should be kept warm, covered with a blanket and, if the weather is cold, with a covered hot water bottle beside it. To pick it up to transport it to the vet, move it gently on to a towel or piece of cloth which can be held taut by two people to lift it.

Bleeding If the bleeding is from a small cut, then all that should be necessary is treatment with an antiseptic followed by regular checking that the wound is healing. For more serious external bleeding on the body, for which you are taking temporary measures before getting the cat to the vet, try to stop the flow by pressing a pad of clean cloth or bandage on to the wound and hold it in place with a bandage or just your hand. If this does not work and you know where the arterial pressure points are on the cat's body, compress the pressure point nearest the injury. If the bleeding is on a limb or the tail, try making a tourniquet out of a length of bandage with a pencil twisted in it. This should be placed on the limb above the wound and must be loosened every 4–5 minutes or so.

Breathing difficulties If the cat's breathing is irregular or has stopped altogether, artificial respiration will be necessary. Check

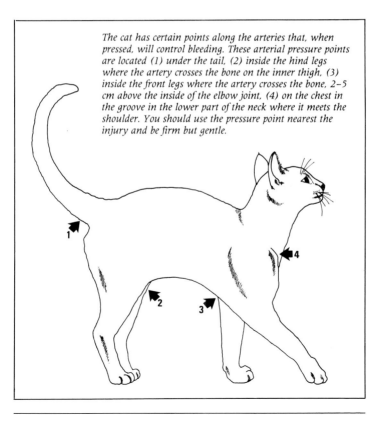

The cat has certain points along the arteries that, when pressed, will control bleeding. These arterial pressure points are located (1) under the tail, (2) inside the hind legs where the artery crosses the bone on the inner thigh, (3) inside the front legs where the artery crosses the bone, 2–5 cm above the inside of the elbow joint, (4) on the chest in the groove in the lower part of the neck where it meets the shoulder. You should use the pressure point nearest the injury and be firm but gentle.

inside the cat's mouth for vomit or an obstruction and clear it, if necessary; lay the cat on its side and, holding the mouth closed, blow steadily into the nostrils for several seconds. Take a breath and repeat until some resistance can be felt or until the chest rises.

If the cat has been taken **unconscious out of water**, hold it head-down by its hind legs and shake it several times to clear water out of its lungs and air passages. The cat should not be held like this for more than 20 seconds. This action may help, too, if the cat has choked on some solid object which you have not been able to dislodge with a spatula, teaspoon handle, or a pair of tweezers.

Burns Cold water and ice are the best temporary remedies for burns. Submerge the cat up to its neck in cold water for at least five minutes, then take it to the vet, applying *no* cream or ointment beforehand, as the vet will only have to scrape it off before treating the cat. If the burns are from chemicals, then once again the best immediate treatment is copious washing with cold water, with the person doing the washing wearing protective rubber gloves. If a cat has received a very small burn, then petroleum jelly may be all that is necessary to put it right.

Heat prostration The recent very warm summers in Britain came as much of a surprise to cats as to their owners and heat prostration became quite common among them. Cats will normally pant or breathe heavily to cool down when they get overheated, but a cat severely affected by heat will be breathing rapidly, perhaps staggering about, and showing its tongue, which will look very red. Once again, the treatment is to immerse the cat in cold water up to its neck for several minutes before taking it to the vet.

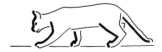

Poisoning Cats can be poisoned by eating poisoned rats or the poison laid down for rats, squirrels and other rodents. They can be poisoned when they lick up car antifreeze carelessly spilled in a garage, strong bleaches, paint strippers and thinners, petrol, turpentine, and many other liquids to be found around the house. And they can be poisoned by eating drugs and pills such as aspirin, paracetamol, anti-depressants and antibiotics. Symptoms include salivating, vomiting, diarrhoea, fits, muscle tremors and a staggering gait. Its back legs may appear paralysed and it may lose consciousness.

The best treatment is to get the cat to the vet as soon as possible, putting it in a dark, quiet place while the vet is contacted. If the poison is known, or suspected, the vet should be told so that antidotes can be prepared; suspect containers should be taken to the vet with the cat. If the vet is not immediately available, and you *know* the poison was rat poison, metaldehyde slug pellets or a drug such as aspirin or barbiturates, and if the cat is conscious, it could be given two teaspoonfuls of a strongish salt water solution (two teaspoons of salt in half a cup of warm water) to make it sick. Never try to make sick a cat which has swallowed alkalines or acids.

Stings If the cat has stood on an insect and been stung, the sting will show up as a hard swelling on the paw. A bee sting should be removed and the paw treated with a weak solution of hydrogen peroxide or a paste of bicarbonate of soda and water; treat wasp stings with vinegar. A vet will have to deal with stings on the mouth or tongue.

Signs Of Illness

Detailed analyses of the illnesses and diseases which can affect cats would be out of place in a book such as this, which does not pretend to be a professional cat-care manual. However, there are numerous signs and pointers to illness in cats which every cat owner should be aware of.

Ill-health in a cat may show up gradually in changes in its appearance and in behaviour which differs from its usual pattern. Its fur may be less sleek than usual and stand up in untidy tufts, its eyes may be dull with the haw showing at the inner corners, and its general pattern of behaviour may be slower, duller and less active than usual. Its appetite can diminish or, in contrast, become voracious.

As cats can become difficult to handle when they are ill, needing to be approached very gently, it is wise, if sickness is suspected, to spend a little time simply watching and listening, from which a great deal can be learnt about a cat's condition.

The eyes – is there any discharge, and, if so, is it clear or cloudy (clear would suggest blocked tear ducts, and cloudy some kind of infection); does the eyeball appear to be protruding, the eyelid not closing or the pupils dilating (any of which could suggest something quite seriously wrong)?

The nose – is it hot and dry rather than cool and moist; is there a nasal discharge (which could be indications of colds, infections or allergic reactions)?

The ears – has the cat been scratching them, is there any wax or pus in the ear, or any discharge from the ear (which could suggest parasites, blockages or infection)?

Breathing – is it difficult or rapid, rather than the even and quiet 25–30 breaths a minute which is normal; is it slow and does it remain slow even when the cat is moved; is it rapid and accompanied by other signs of something wrong (all indications that the cat should be taken to the vet as soon as possible)?

If a major illness strikes suddenly, the warning signs will be obvious: repeated vomiting, constipation or its opposite, diarrhoea, over a longish period; abnormal or difficult breathing; bleeding from one of the body's orifices; collapse. The vet should be consulted at once.

Taking A Cat's Temperature

It is often helpful to be able to tell the vet over the telephone if a cat has a temperature. A cat's normal temperature is around 38.6°C (101.5°F). A temperature above about 38.9°C (102°F) indicates a fever.

Two people are needed to check a cat's temperature, one to hold the cat still and quiet and one to take the temperature. The most effective place to take a cat's temperature is the rectum, since temperatures taken under the cat's foreleg or in the groin are not very reliable. Thus, a blunt-ended rectal thermometer is essential. The mercury bolt end should be coated lightly with petroleum jelly or vegetable oil and the thermometer shaken to get the mercury level down. Then the cat's tail is lifted with one hand and the thermometer inserted gently into the anus (immediately below the tail) with the other, to a distance of about 2.5 cm (1 inch) along the length of the thermometer. It needs to be held gently in place for one minute to obtain a correct reading.

Feeling The Pulse

A cat's pulse can be checked by placing the fingers (not the thumb: it contains a pulse of its own) over the femoral artery which is high on the inside of the cat's thigh, at the point where the artery crosses the thigh bone. What should be felt in a healthy cat at rest is a regular and strong pulse rate of 100–120 beats a minute; though it will vary somewhat from this depending on the size of the cat. Since even lifting a cat up on to a table or bench to check its pulse can cause the rate to gallop for a time, it is best to leave to experts the making of any long-term conclusions from a cat's pulse rate.

The Carers

Scientists have quite recently discovered something that cat lovers have always known: owning a cat is good for you. A number of scientific studies have been carried out in recent years on the nature of the human/companion animal bond, and their results have pinpointed the ways in which having a cat about the house can do people good. Pet owners live longer than non-pet owners, scientists say, while stroking a cat can lower blood pressure and heartbeat rates, producing a calming effect on the person doing the stroking. New dog and cat owners show dramatic improvements in their mental and physical wellbeing compared with non-pet owners, according to studies in Britain and the USA, and heart attack patients who own a dog or a cat have a significantly higher chance of surviving the attack than those who do not.

Along with this increasing awareness of the important part cats can play in human wellbeing, there has developed a greater understanding, at least among professional health workers, of the effects living with people can have on animals.

When the world's popular press reported that Jane Fonda was paying $600 a week to have her cat treated by a psychiatrist, there were probably many readers who shrugged the news off as only what you'd expect from a Hollywood movie star. But animal behaviourists would have known better, for psychiatry for cats and dogs is becoming big business, and not just in California, home of many mind-improvement schemes and fads. As a book recently published in Britain, which aroused more interest than most cat books, made clear, cats on their own do not need psychiatrists (or animal behaviourists, as they are more often called in Britain). It is the cat-in-the-family and its relationship with the members of its human family that may need psychiatric help.

In *Do Cats Need Shrinks?*, animal behaviourist Peter Neville identified several basic problem areas in the cat/family relation-

'A house without a cat, and a well-fed, well-petted and properly revered cat, may be a perfect house, perhaps, but how can it prove its title?' remarked Mark Twain. If this charming watercolour of a cottage interior is any indication, the artist J. M. W. Turner agreed with the sentiment.

ship. There are cats which become over-attached to their owners; cats which develop a phobia towards one member of the family; cats which up sticks and leave home – though they may just move to the bottom of the garden and refuse to come back into the house; cats which suddenly become aggressive and despotic, or very destructive; cats which begin to show the insecurities of old age; and – a fairly common problem – cats which suddenly take to spraying in the house. (Mr Neville cited the cat that persistently sprayed a picture of a tsar and tsarina of Russia, standing on the banister rail to do it!)

All these are problems an animal behaviourist can help and even overcome, although he needs to talk with owners as well as taking their cats in hand. Most responsible animal behaviourists require cats to be referred to them from vets; indeed, vets should be the first

to be consulted over behaviour problems, since they are themselves very experienced in dealing with many of them, anyway. There is also the Association of Pet Behaviour Consultants, 50 Pall Mall, London SW1, who can give worried cat owners the names and addresses of members' practices.

It is not just the psychiatrist who is turning his attention to animals. In our caring society, animals are being included in the caring provided by many different workers in areas of mental and physical health.

Physiotherapists can often be of as much use in animal rehabilitation as in human. Members of the Society of Chartered Physiotherapists in Animal Therapy use with animals the same treatments including ultrasound and laser treatment, that work to repair human bones, muscles and other physical problem areas. Given the right conditions, dogs, cats, horses, smaller pets and even birds may all be helped by physiotherapy. As with animal behaviourists, physiotherapists who work with animals are best contacted via a vet.

Acupuncture is another area of complementary medicine that can work well with some animal problems. The Chinese have been proving this for centuries: ancient Chinese health manuals show acupuncture points for horses and elephants. There is an Association of British Veterinary Acupuncture, and a growing number of vets are using it as therapy. Acupuncture can be effective in relieving such conditions as arthritis in dogs and cats, even helping animals which have become virtually immobile to walk without pain.

Then there are dentists who work with animals, including some who have a human dentistry practice three or four days a week and work on animals' teeth, often in their local veterinary practice, for another day or two. Vets themselves regularly carry out dental work, too. Having good teeth is as important for animals as it is for people. Cats can get large cavities in teeth and bad gum inflammation, but there is no need to suffer long-term effects now that fillings and crowns for teeth have become technologically possible for animals.

The most important carer in the human/animal relationship remains the vet. There are something like 10,000 vets in Britain, who will all have gone through an enormously demanding six-year course of study at one of the country's six veterinary schools before finding a place in one of the near-3000 practices to be found throughout the country.

Contrary to what we have all learned from the stories of that very famous vet, 'James Herriot', few vets actually work in the sort of 'mixed' surgery, catering for all creatures, great and small, that kept James, the Farnon brothers and the rest of them so busy on BBC television for many years. Most veterinary practices today concentrate on 'small animals' or 'large animals'. We cannot take our cats to really specialist, feline-only clinics, as many cat owners can do in the United States and Australia, because the Royal College of Veterinary Surgeons does not permit practices to become so specialized.

Scientists, on the other hand, can specialize, and feline medicine has made enormous advances in recent years. The University of Bristol Veterinary School's work in feline medicine has been so detailed and wide-ranging as to attract attention from all over the world. It has also inspired two feline charities, the Cats Protection League and the Feline Advisory Bureau, to establish scholarships which enable veterinary surgeons to undertake a year's study of feline medical topics within the School's department of veterinary medicine.

More recently, one of Britain's biggest manufacturers of small animal vaccines has funded a similar scholarship at the Liverpool University Veterinary School. The manufacturer probably found the money a little more easily than the charities: the purchase of drugs is a large slice of the £500 million or so we spend on our pets at the vet in Britain.

Veterinary surgery can be enormously expensive, because the science and technology behind the work is costly. It can cost £800 to replace a dog's hip bone, £400 to put a pacemaker in a smaller animal. For some people, this poses a moral question: should we spend so much money on caring for animals?

'Yes,' say the vets. Dr Dick White, lecturer in small animal soft tissue surgery at Cambridge University's Veterinary School, put the issue in context in an interview with a national newspaper: 'Since we maintain them in a very artificial environment for our own needs and pleasures, we have a responsibility to look after them. The answer is to do the best possible job you can.'

Zoonoses Explained

These are diseases which can be passed from animals to humans. Cat ailments which can be so transmitted are rabies, ringworm and worms, cat scratch fever and toxoplasmosis. The last named, caused by a parasite in the cat's gut which gets into its faeces, is rare in humans but is a risk to pregnant women and to their babies.

Sensible precautions should prevent these infections being picked up from cats: hands should be washed after touching a pet; pregnant women and children should be particularly wary of touching a cat's droppings. Gardeners working in neighbourhoods with cats should always wear gloves when working in the soil; children's sandpits should be kept covered when not in use, since cats think they are splendid litter trays; clean all bites and scratches from cats at once and treat them with antiseptic; cat scratch fever causes pustules to develop at the site of the scratch, so any sign of these means a quick visit to the doctor for drugs to clear up the infection before it becomes deep-rooted. Finally, always quarantine cats with ringworm.

Cats & Society

Legal Niceties

In 10th-century Wales, codes of law were promulgated in different parts of the country and they all included sections concerning the value of cats. In Howel the Good's Codes enacted for South Wales, a legally defined hamlet was listed as nine buildings, one plough, one kiln, one churn, one cat, one cock, one bull and one herdsman. The Code also ruled that if a cat was caught mousing in someone's flax garden, the cat's owner should pay the damage.

In both the north Wales and south-east Wales Codes, the essential qualities of a cat were said to include perfect ears, eyes and claws, the ability to kill mice skilfully and the ability to bring up kittens well and not eat them; in the southern code it was also made clear that a good cat was one that 'be not caterwauling on every new moon'.

Although the legal position of cats changed considerably over the following centuries, man's mistaken belief in his ability to control the behaviour of cats, even to stopping them howling at each other in the moonlight, lived on in laws right up to the 20th century.

A present-day law in the state of Ohio, USA, requires all domestic animals out after lighting-up time to wear tail-lights. The cat is a domestic animal, but a particularly independent one. It is as unlikely to wear a tail-light happily after dark as it is to refrain from caterwauling at night or obey a curfew, both of which limitations have been legally put upon them from time to time.

There is a provision in the state laws of Idaho that schoolchildren should be taught about 'the destructiveness of the common house cat to bird life and . . . the necessity of protecting the same against the said common house cat'. In other statutes of the Union bird lovers have persuaded their local governments that cats should be belled and that people should not be allowed to keep cats and birds in the same household. Dog lovers in one state managed to persuade their legislature to pass a law which forbade cats to disturb dogs 'in any fashion'.

One should not assume from all this that the state legislatures of the United States are not on the side of the cat. On the contrary, cats come firmly within the scope of the animal anti-cruelty laws which all states have enacted. Though some of these laws are considerably less severe than others, things have on the whole been looking up for cats in recent years. In Florida in 1989, for instance, animal cruelty laws were toughened to include a maximum three-year jail penalty for anyone convicted of cruelty to animals, including cats.

When Ronald Reagan was Governor of California, he signed into state law in 1973 a bill under which a person could be sent to prison for kicking or injuring another person's cat. Governor Reagan probably needed no persuasion to sign the bill; with three cats living on their California ranch, Ronald and Nancy Reagan are known to be something of cat people.

In Britain, cat owners have a fairly low-risk relationship with the courts. The law has come to recognize the independent nature of cats. They are the only domestic animal which cannot be accused of trespass and their owners cannot, on the whole, be held responsible for their cats' actions (unless negligence on the part of the owner can be proved).

A 1990 court case agreed, in a particular instance, with the latter piece of common law. The owner of a collie-labrador cross called Sheba took the owner of a fluffy grey cat called Smokey to court, accusing Smokey of ambushing Sheba and savagely attacking her. Smokey ambled home after the alleged attack unscathed, but poor Sheba had lost a toe from a back paw and the subsequent veterinary bills totalled £350, which Sheba's owner claimed in his case in the Aldershot and Farnham County Court in Surrey.

'It is a question of whether under English law, the owner has liability for the actions of his cat,' said Sheba's owner outside the court. 'Because it happened to a dog . . . people are treating it as a bit of a joke.' Smokey's owner thought that if it was a joke, it was one in poor taste. 'I was accused of harbouring a dangerous animal. There was no way Smokey could have done it. She is extremely timid and frightened of loud noises.' In the event, having heard both sides of the case, the court decided against awarding Sheba's owner the veterinary costs.

Although the British Parliament has passed some ten Dogs Acts or Dogs (Amendments) Acts since the Dog Licences Act of 1867, culminating, to date, in the abolition of the dog licence fee in Britain in 1990, no act devoted solely to the welfare of cats has ever been passed in Britain.

Cats are, of course, covered by British anti-cruelty laws. The first Act of Parliament protecting domestic animals was passed in Britain in 1822. Though it applied mainly to cattle and other farm animals, its provisions were used later in the century by the Royal Society for the Protection of Animals – formed in 1824 and given royal patronage by Queen Victoria in 1840 – to bring successful prosecutions for cruelty to cats, as well as other animals. People convicted of cruelty – such as the case in an early RSPCA annual report of a cat stabbed repeatedly with a butcher's stick fitted with two iron hooks – could be fined 10–40 shillings (50 pence–£2) or given 7–14 days' hard labour in the House of Correction in Brixton, London.

The Protection of Animals Act, 1911, hailed at the time it was passed as an 'animals' charter', covered almost every conceivable form of animal ill-treatment and greatly increased the severity of the punishments courts could hand down, including the power to deprive an owner found guilty of a cruelty offence of ownership of the animal. Under the 1911 act, cruelty to a cat could include such forms of ill-treatment as kicking, torturing, infuriating or terrifying it; causing it to be carried in such a way as to cause it unnecessary suffering; wilfully administering any poison or injurious drug; permitting it to be subjected to any operation performed without due care and humanity; selling, offering for sale or giving away any grain or seed rendered poisonous; or putting on any land or building any poison, fluid or edible matter (not being grain or seed) rendered poisonous.

The domestic cat also comes within the scope of numerous other Acts of Parliament. Under the Sale of Goods Act, 1893, a domestic cat is considered to be a chattel for sale purposes, and the general law covering the sale of goods therefore applies to the cat. In a pet shop, as in any other shop, *caveat emptor* applies, and it is up to the purchaser of a kitten, say, to make sure that the animal is free of defects before taking it out of the shop. If the kitten appears healthy in the shop, but becomes ill shortly after it is taken home, no redress can be expected from the pet shop owner who could not be

expected to know a healthy-looking kitten was, in fact, ill or harbouring infection.

The Animals (Anaesthetics) Act of 1919 made it unlawful for
certain operations to be performed on cats without a general anaes-
thetic sufficiently powerful to prevent the cats feeling any pain.
Neutering operations were included in this Act.

The Pet Animals Acts, 1951, did much to regulate the way in
which pet shops are run, placing them within the authority of local
councils who are empowered to issue licences for operating pet
shops under certain conditions. Local authorities have the power to
inspect pet shops to ensure that they are kept clean, well ventilated
and free of fire hazards, that they are adequately heated and lit and
that the animals in them are supplied with food and drink and not
sold at too young an age. This Act also forbade the sale of cats in the
street or in any other public places, apart from properly licensed
market stalls, and banned the sale of cats to anyone under the age
of 12 years.

The Pest Act, 1954, prohibited the use of certain kinds of spring
trap for catching vermin and made the sale and ownership of them
illegal. Since cats were often caught in these traps, the Act thus pre-
vented much suffering among cats.

The offence of cruelty within the meaning of the 1911 Protection
of Animals Act was extended to the abandoning of animals,
including cats, 'whether permanently or not, in circumstances
likely to cause the cat unnecessary suffering', by the Abandonment
of Animals Act, 1960.

Another animal business to be subject to licensing by local authorities is the boarding cattery. The 1963 Animal Boarding Establishments Act empowered local authorities to inspect such establishments from time to time, after they have issued a licence which they do on the basis of much the same inspection procedure as for pet shops. Boarding cattery licences have to be renewed annually and the management must keep a register of all cats admitted, with the names and addresses of owners. It is also the management's responsibility to ensure that infectious diseases do not get spread through the cattery. Scrupulous cleanliness is obviously one way of preventing infections, but most catteries also insist on all boarders arriving with valid vaccination certificates.

The Theft Act, 1968, once again deems the domestic cat to be a chattel and therefore something which can be stolen. If a cat is stolen, lost or a stray and gets taken in by a concerned cat lover, it remains the property of its original owner, who may claim it back as long as six years after the original theft and/or loss. Note, though, that feral and wild cats are not legal chattels and therefore cannot be stolen.

The Road Traffic Act, 1972, does not include cats in its definition of an animal which, if struck and injured by a motor car, must be reported by the car's driver to the police or other responsible person 'having reasonable grounds for requiring' the name and address of the driver and of the car's owner and its registration number. Animals which drivers must report hitting are a horse, cattle, ass, mule, sheep, pig, goat and dog. But don't forget that 1911 Protection of Animals Act; if you did hit a cat and drove on without stopping to see if you could help it, you could be reported for causing the animal 'unneccessary suffering', contrary to the 1911 Act.

Talking about cats and cars: a clause in the Road Code makes it clear that it is an offence for a cat to be left unrestrained in a car if the only other occupant is the driver.

A recent Act which has helped cat owners sleep easier in their beds at night is the Animals (Scientific Procedures) Act, 1986. Among other things, this Act provided that no cat could be used in experiments on living animals which had not been bred at a designated breeding establishment holding a certificate issued by the responsible government department. Thus it was hoped the nasty business of stealing cats to sell them to scientific establishments would be stamped out.

Since a cat cannot be guilty of trespass, your neighbour has no redress if your cat scratches up his garden bulbs or strops his claws on the fence; on the other hand, you have no redress if your cat is made ill by eating the slug pellets the neighbour has scattered among his bulbs; the cat must bear the consequences of its actions.

Insurance

When Downing Street staff replaced Wilberforce, No. 10's famous mousecatcher and cat-in-residence for 14 years, with black-and-white Humphrey in 1990, they took out insurance for him – up to a million pounds for third party liability, so it was reported. Assuming they had taken out a sufficiently comprehensive insurance policy, Humphrey should not now be a big cost to the nation's purse as animal insurance policies these days can cover all sorts of eventualities.

Handsome black-and-white tom cat, Humphrey, got himself a job as rodent operative in the Downing Street Cabinet Office complex simply by walking in off the street in 1990. When off duty he shares an office with accommodation officer Mr Kevin Lapwood, shown here holding Humphrey for the benefit of press photographers.

Because most of us do not have to pay large doctors' or hospital bills, relying as we can on the National Health Service, veterinary medical and surgical costs can come as a considerable shock, one which the right insurance cover can ease considerably. And they will provide it for a not unreasonable charge; most cats can be found basic insurance cover for around £25–£40 a year.

It is advisable to shop around among the various companies which offer animal insurance to get the one which best suits the circumstances of both owner and cat.

Some insurance schemes put an upper limit on the amount they will pay out on any one illness or course of treatment. Most will deduct an initial sum from each claim before paying out. Some companies will pay veterinary bills direct, while others make the cats' owners pay the bills then reclaim the costs from the insurance company, which could take some time to finalize.

Many schemes, as well as providing cover for illness, also offer third party liability and will pay cattery fees in the event of an owner being rushed to hospital, leaving the cat uncared for. Some schemes will pay replacement costs if a cat is killed, lost or stolen and may even cover the cost of advertising the loss and offering a reward.

Insurance companies will not accept for insurance cats aged eight and over, and may not continue the insurance policy after the cat becomes elderly. This is a point which should be cleared up before any policy is taken out.

Since insurance schemes do not cover such basic preventive treatment as inoculations or special diets, nor the cost of neutering or spaying, many owners, hoping the cats will not need the vet's services for much else, decide against insurance. Knowing about the sort of things cats might get up to that insurance companies will cover, might make them think again. Here are two stories from the files of the Pet Plan Insurance Company:

An 8 kg (18 lb) moggie from England climbed the family's Christmas tree and toppled it, spraining his leg and damaging his eye. The cat also damaged the Christmas tree more than just a little. The insurance company paid out nearly £100 for the damage caused to cat and tree.

That same Christmas somewhere else in England a Siamese cat chewed up its family's Christmas tree lights beyond repair.

Cats At War

As this book was being written, it was clear that there would soon be a major war in the Middle East. On the day war finally came to the Gulf, newspapers noted that one small refugee from the conflict had already made it to safety in Britain: a stowaway Saudi Arabian cat had turned up after a month-long voyage in a cargo ship. It had been found in a crate of leather skins and had survived, as is the way of cats in such conditions, by licking condensation inside the crate. Rescued by the Cats Protection League from the threat of being put down under Britain's strict rabies prevention law, the cat was put into quarantine and was also found a home in Somerset after its time in quarantine. Its new owners named it Jeddah.

But what if Britain had been directly involved in the conflict? Would there have been time to worry about Jeddah? Do cats get forgotten in wartime, left to take their chances? Stories of cats in Britain and elsewhere during World War II are reassuring.

Even at the highest levels of government, cats had honoured places in wartime Britain. The place of Winston Churchill's cat was, more often than not, on the Prime Minister's bed keeping the great man's feet warm. Even the war cabinet had an official mouse exterminator, called Jumbo. A letter from an official in the Central Statistical Office, written in 1942, showed a sense of humour in describing the cat as suffering from 'eatoomuchitis' and unable to 'follow his employment'. Five days later Jumbo died, presumably from overeating – not a common occurrence in wartime food-rationed Britain!

Cats had not been forgotten in the careful husbanding of Britain's food resources. At the end of 1941, the Minister of Food announced that cats 'engaged in work of national importance' should have an allowance of powdered milk, taken from stock damaged in hand-ling and no longer fit for human consumption. To qualify, cats would have to be 'engaged in keeping down mice and rats in ware-houses in which at least 250 tons of food or animal feeding stuffs are stored'. *The Daily Telegraph* considered this attempt to measure the service given by working cats to the war effort a 'significant step'.

The Cat, the long-established official journal of the Cats Protection League, printed a piece in 1942 designed to help cat owners think calmly about what to do should the enemy land:

'That dreadful question of what to do in a sudden invasion! I am haunted by the thought of frightened semi-hysterical cat owners trying to put an end to their cats in a few panicky minutes . . . At the first alarm, I shall open all the doors and windows and trust to my cat's wonderful instincts. If the enemy reaches the house I am certain he will keep away, and as certain that he will come back when they have gone. Should I be killed in the meantime, the neighbours within reach, the police, the veterinary surgeon, the usual tradesmen, all have his description, and injunctions to look out for him. We shall not all be killed, and he will be taken in and sent to a prearranged place where he will be put to sleep. If I survive, he will rejoin me when the noise of war has passed else-where.'

A cat called **Faith** was awarded a medal after the War for her brav-ery during the height of the Blitz in London. Faith had been adopted as the church cat of St Augustine and St Faith, a church in the shadow of St Paul's Cathedral. She gave birth to a kitten in the summer of 1940 and tended it lovingly in a room in the Rector's house until one day, early in September, she removed her kitten from its basket and carried it down three floors to the bottom of the house, putting it carefully into a recess in a wall. Several times the Rector carried the kitten back upstairs and each time Faith took it back down again. Eventually, the Rector let Faith have her way and had her basket carried down to the recess. Three nights later, the City of London suffered a heavy bombing raid, during which St Augustine's and the Rectory were hit, the latter being reduced to a ruin. As luck would have it, the Rector was away from home that night and returned in the morning to find his house all but destroyed and his cat surely dead. Still, he searched in the rubble as best he could, calling to Faith. Then, to his enormous relief, he heard the kitten mew. The Rector called to the firemen still at the site and together they moved enough of the wreckage to clear a way to the recess. There Faith was sitting, calm and unruffled, her kitten between her paws.

When the director of the People's Dispensary for Sick Animals heard Faith's story five years later, he decided that although she was not eligible for the PDSA's prestigious Dickin Medal, she must be honoured, and in October 1945 a medal and certificate were presented to Faith. The medal was engraved 'From the PDSA to Faith of St Augustine's, Watling Street, E.C. for steadfast courage in the Battle of London, September 9th, 1940'. The certificate was hung in the chapel of St Augustine's Tower, which was all that remained of the church after the War and which was later incorporated into the new building of the Cathedral Choir School.

During the Blitz, Faith sat guarding her kitten in a city of London church, steadfast against the bombs, fire and falling masonry that threatened her. The PDSA awarded her a special silver medal for bravery and a plaque was erected in her honour in St Augustine's, city of London.

The cat's ability to sense trouble came into its own during the war, and there are countless stories of how people found their cats' behaviour a quicker guide to danger than the air raid sirens. For instance, cats would be seen moving their kittens to places of safety, or taking themselves off to a suitable shelter minutes before the bombs began to fall. There is even note of a cat which quickly learned to distinguish between the sound of an enemy aeroplane and a British one. When a German plane flew over – and the cat would hear it a good half minute before its owner – it would jump under the heavy cooker in the kitchen; British planes it simply ignored.

The long-drawn-out agony of the siege of Stalingrad during World War II produced a feline hero called Mourka, whose bravery was celebrated in a leader in *The Times* in January 1943. The cat carried messages concerning the whereabouts of German gun emplacements from Russian scouts on one side of a war-torn street in the city to a house on the other side. The suggestion that the cat crossed the street so readily because there was food in the kitchen of the house on the other side, *The Times* writer dismissed as the 'cavilling peculiar to vulgar minds . . . The name of Mourka must never be coupled with a breath of doubt. He has shown himself worthy of Stalingrad and, whether cat or man, there can be no higher praise.'

Dear Editor

If no one ever wrote books about cats, published thousands of cat calendars and greeting cards, or produced millions of cat food cans to end up buried deep in municipal rubbish dumps, future historians and social archaeologists would still be able to gauge the depth of the cat's acceptance into our way of life by reading the correspondence columns in newspapers and magazines. Just a few months of keeping an eye on such newpapers and magazines as came into view produced a varied and entertaining haul of comment and anecdote on the theme of cats.

The reactions of small children to cats provided material for many letters from fond mothers to their favourite magazines. Two samples: a small boy, chastised for carrying three little kittens by their tails, replied indignantly, 'Well, I'm holding them by their stems!', and a little girl explained to her mother how she knew the electricity had come on again after a power cut: 'That's easy: the cat's started purring again.'

Entrances and exits get a look in. There were two versions of the story of how Sir Isaac Newton cut a hole in a door in his house so that his cat could get in and out, and then followed it up with a second, smaller hole for a new kitten, thus demonstrating that even great minds can go loopy over cats. And there was this notice from a Yorkshire newspaper, sent to a women's magazine: 'For Sale, lovely cross-bred puppies. Mother a Jack Russell. Father came in through the cat flap.'

Then there was the lady who warned readers of another magazine of an unforeseen consequence of getting a new cat. 'I hadn't seen a mouse in the house for years and years. Then I got Smudge. She catches mice outside, brings them into the house and then lets them go free. So now, I've got a houseful.'

Cats may bring more than mice into the house. A letter to *Country Life* told the magazine's readers how to catch shrews brought in unharmed by domestic cats – 'a distressing habit'. All that was needed was a pair of Wellington boots, familiar items to *Country Life* readers, placed alongside the skirting board on either side of the shrew. 'When disturbed from its refuge behind a chest or cupboard, it is certain to run straight into the open end of the boot. It can then be taken out of doors and liberated.'

A report in *The Guardian* that a man had received compensation from Christchurch (Hants) Borough Council for the injuries he received to his back when he fell after treading on a sleeping cat, brought in an indignant letter from the owner of three cats, demanding 'the cat's side of the story'. Had anyone considered the mental anguish suffered by the cat at being so rudely awakened?

Taking tongue out of cheek, the writer went on to ask, more pertinently, why the council had paid out at all on injuries caused by an innocent animal: 'was there a notice prohibiting cats from sleeping in that particular place, for instance?'

Readers of *The Times* appear to be a very cat-conscious lot, to judge by their letters. There was a series of letters headed 'Give a Dog . . .' about people whose surnames were those of the birds and beasts. From these, readers learned that there were 57 'Catts' listed in the Brighton and area telephone directory; that resident in Wiltshire were an A. Catt and an M. A. D. Dog; and that Mr Bob Katt was delighted that his father had 'mercifully avoided' calling him Thomas – a fate he visited on Bob's younger brother instead; that the Kit-Cat Club was founded in 1703 at the Cat and Fiddle tavern, near Temple Bar, kept by one Christopher Cat; that there was not long ago a Catt's restaurant in Deal, Kent; and that the cat in the well-known political lampoon from Richard III's reign,

> 'The rat, the cat and Lovell our dog,
> Rule all England under an hog',

referred to one of Richard's counsellors, Sir William Catesby.

An earlier series of letters to *The Times*, called 'Credit Where Due', was about literary dedications, prompted by John Grigg, Chairman of the London Library, who remarked in an article that he could think of only one book dedicated to an animal. Naturally, *The Times'* readers were quick to put him right, coming up with several animal dedicatees, including a camel called Feri n'Gashi. A reader noted that the eminent Latinists, D. R. Shackleton and Konrad Muller, had dedicated important works in their discipline to their cats, in Latin, since 1965. Another reader wrote to point out that Ms Frances Simpson's book, *Cats for Pleasure and Profit*, was dedicated

> 'To the many kind friends,
> Known and unknown,
> That I have made in
> Pussydom'.

This reader perhaps missed Mr Grigg's point: it is fairly commonplace to dedicate books *about* animals *to* animals, but much rarer to dedicate books on other subjects to them. Indeed, Mr Grigg could quickly have found several examples of the former on the shelves of his own library, had he wished. Here is a charming one from *Cats Beneath Covers: A Bibliography of Books About Cats* by Sidney Denham:

> *To*
> *Yum-Yum*
> *and all the*
> *other cats whose stories*
> *are written only in the hearts*
> *of those who shared*
> *their lives.*

It's A Cat's World

Cats are always in the news, and for a wide range of reasons. In 1990 an adorable tabby kitten appeared on a **British** first-class **postage stamp**. It was one of a set of four stamps issued to commemorate the 150th anniversary of the granting of a Royal Charter to the Royal Society for the Prevention of Cruelty to Animals. This was the first time a domestic cat had been portrayed solo on a British stamp. There was a black-and-white kitten on the 16 pence 1983 Christmas stamp, but he had to share the space with chimney pots representing the Three Wise Men, and the 31 pence stamp in the 1986 Nature Conservation series showed a Wild Cat (*Felis silvestris*).

This fluffy tabby kitten appeared on one of a series of animal-life stamps issued in 1990 in Britain to mark the 150th anniversary of the Royal Society for the Prevention of Cruelty to Animals.

A **festival of British music, arts, trade and industry** was held in Kiev, in the **Soviet Union**. Included in it was an exhibition featuring a typical British family living in a typical British house, all based on recent government statistics on what represents the 'average' in our country. Naturally, the family included a pet cat, a tabby called George.

The **stray cats** of **France** had an amazing windfall in 1990: art gallery owners Lucien and Marcelle Bourdon auctioned off 54 paintings, including a Modigliani, to raise £64 million which they intend using to make provision for their own cats and the tens of thousands of stray cats in France. The Bourdons plan to form their own organizations to distribute their millions and to use established animal welfare bodies in France. There are plenty of cats for the money to be spent on. There are estimated to be 40,000 stray cats in France at any one time, with thousands more in Paris. An inoculation programme in north-east France, where rabies is beginning to spread through the cat population, could be a good starting point for spending the Bourdon millions.

The **Feline Advisory Bureau** of **Britain** also had a windfall in 1990 – a mere £1 million in this instance, but nonetheless welcome. It was left to the Bureau by a cat-lover on condition that it ensured that his two Siamese cats were cared for 'in the manner to which they had become accustomed'.

A cat has helped Mr Snowy Farr, from Cambridge, England, raise £27,000 for charity and donate 17 guide dogs for the blind over the past ten years. Every Saturday Mr Farr takes his cat and a few mice to Cambridge's main market square and puts on a money-raising performance, involving his cat sitting on his top hat and the mice running round the brim. 'Only God, myself and my animals tell me what to do, and that's how it all started,' Snowy was reported to say. 'We have a great time, everyone crowding around playing with the cat and having fun.' Eccentric, maybe, but very worthwhile.

The cat looks more apprehensive than the mice as Mr Snowy Farr begins one of his regular charity-supporting performances in Cambridge's main market square. In 10 years, Mr Farr, cat and mice have raised enough money to donate 17 guide dogs to the blind.

To Mr Robert Fisk, *The Independent* newspaper's correspondent in war-troubled Saudi Arabia, **Beirut** beckons like an outpost of heaven, he told the paper's readers in 1990. And Mr Fisk's idea of heaven? – 'An apartment over the sea with chilled wine in the fridge and a voracious and affectionate cat called Walter – named after the news editor of a well-known international newspaper.'

Burglars burgle better when dressed as cats, or maybe they just merge better with the Hallowe'en crowds. A man dressed as a black cat robbed a tropical fish store in Las Vegas last Hallowe'en. He grabbed the money but left the fish alone, despite the fact that he was wearing a complete black cat outfit, with a green mask. 'He even had a tail,' said an astonished police spokesman.

On The Town

Cats add a certain *je ne sais quoi* – a calm sophistication, perhaps – to establishments they choose to grace with their presence. Which is

Tabitha is the cat-in-residence at the Phoenix Theatre, Charing Cross Road, seen here with Nicholas Parsons.

no doubt why so many of the cultural gathering places of London – theatres, clubs and bars – have become home to some well-known cats.

Cats are considered to be bringers of good luck to theatres, so it is not surprising that a number of London's great theatres have had cats living in.

Doyen of London's **theatre cats** is **Beerbohm**, named after the great Edwardian actor-manager, Herbert Beerbohm Tree. Beerbohm was born in Herbert Beerbohm Tree's home base, **Her Majesty's Theatre** in the Haymarket, but was transferred to the **Globe** in Shaftesbury Avenue, where he has been an active member of the staff for over 12 years now. A handsome tabby, Beerbohm has even managed the occasional unrehearsed stage appearance, most notably during a Hinge and Bracket show.

Beerbohm's nearest colleague is **Fleur**, who lives up the Avenue at the **Lyric**. Fleur is a less exuberant cat than Beerbohm and has never shown any inclination to take to the boards.

Drury Lane Theatre's cat in the spotlight for a time was **Ambrose**. Always immaculately turned out in black jacket and white front, Ambrose achieved brief fame when he strolled across the stage during an evening's performance of *A Chorus Line*, to applause from the audience.

An even closer appearance by cat and performer took place at the old **St James Theatre** (long since pulled down, despite a spirited and famous objection by Vivien Leigh from the public gallery of the House of Lords). The pianist, Paderewski, gave his first per-

At the Apollo, Polly and Victoria *pose with* Starlight Express *star George Channing.*

formance in London at the St James in 1890. As he walked on stage, he saw a cat sitting out front and remarked to it, 'Wish me luck!' The cat jumped on to his lap and stayed there, purring, until the end of the great pianist's first group of pieces. Needless to say, the concert was a great success.

John Van Druten's play, *Bell, Book and Candle*, requires a Siamese cat to play **Pyewacket**. London's first production of the play was at the **Connaught Theatre**, where the management, after auditions, eventually hired two Siamese cats, one to play the part of Pyewacket, and his brother, ostensibly to act as understudy, but really just to be a backstage companion in case of stage fright. The Connaught's own cat had the pleasantly ordinary name of Mac, and it is said that after Mac disappeared one day, the Connaught's fortunes gradually faded.

If cats become part of the show in theatres, they can seem like one of the members in the more restrained, and private, world of the London club. The cat at the **Naval and Military Club** in Piccadilly (more familiarly known as the In and Out because of the large 'In' and 'Out' on its stone gateposts) is called **Fudge**. A beautiful tabby, Fudge rid the club of its mouse problem in her early days, but is now taking old age at her leisure.

Across Hyde Park and down in the more artistic world of the Kings Road and Chelsea, the cat-in-residence, in bar and garden, at the **Chelsea Arts Club** is the splendid marmalade-coloured **Orlando**. The Chelsea Arts Club, founded in 1890 as a club for the 'bohemian in character', has always had a cat. Its most famous one was **Fred**, who lived at the club for 16 years and was eventually made a full member. So, if somewhere as bohemian as the Chelsea Arts Club keeps its membership list in detail, Fred's name will be there along with such famous ones as James McNeill Whistler, Walter Sickert, Augustus John, Alfred Munnings, John Ireland and Laurie Lee.

What Is A Catperson?

The world, some people will tell you, is divided up into dogpeople and catpeople. Furthermore, they will go on, you are either one or the other, you cannot be both. It is not just a question of liking one more than the other, it is a question of deep affinity. The point is, some people cannot recognize their own deepest affinity.

James Thurber thought he knew. 'Now I am not a cat man, but a dog man, and all felines can tell this at a glance – a sharp, vindictive glance,' he wrote in a superbly funny piece called 'My Senegalese Birds and Siamese Cats'. Thurber appeared to think that it is women who are catpeople: 'If you ever see a Siamese cat thumbing a ride by the side of a lonely road, you can be sure it was surreptitiously put out of the car by a dog man and not a cat woman.' But he ended his story with a portrait of himself haunted by one of his wife's Siamese cats, killed in a flash of black and a gleam of teeth by a Scottish terrier bitch whose puppies the cat had strayed too close to, and now returned to earth as a 'lithe silken female cat human'. So, at least at one point in his life, Thurber was obsessed by cats. But we must agree with him, that he was not a catperson.

Bernard Levin *is* a catperson. He is not obsessed by cats, but he loves them and in his book *Enthusiasms* he explains why.

'I respected them before I loved them, and have never thought of them as four-legged human beings, or believed that they are on earth to amuse us, or that they see the world through our eyes, or think in our categories . . .

'Cats will let us love them, in fact they plainly wish us to, but they will not love us in return, though many of us delude ourselves that they do. On the other hand, they do not pretend to reciprocate our feelings, they make no promises that they cannot or will not keep, and they swear no empty vows; better so, much better . . .

'I love the feel of cats, from the firm skull between the firm ears to the undulating tail with its amazing strength and versatility. I love their freedom from treachery; a creature which makes clear that it will pledge no permanent loyalty cannot be accused of breaking its vows, and there is nothing in the history of cats to match those of dogs which, after years of fidelity, without warning turn and rend their owners. I love their intelligence and their waywardness, their persistence and their willingness to abandon it if it should prove fruitless (whoever heard of an obstinate cat?). I love their eyes, the most beautiful eyes in the animal kingdom, with their rainbow of flecks among the colours . . .

'But above all, perhaps, I love the detachment of cats, their willingness to be loved but not to respond beyond a very clearly defined point. There is no danger in loving cats, even in loving one particular cat.'

Like Bernard Levin, **Alan Coren** writes regularly for *The Times* newspaper, entertaining and informing its readers with his reflections on everyday life. In the following piece *The Times* readers were told how Mr Coren, starting out as an unbeliever, was taught by a cat that he was a catperson.

'None of this would be a problem if the cat didn't have a cerebrum. Because it has a cerebrum, it is capable of rational thought, and because it is capable of rational thought, it may well have a reason for doing what it does. I need to discover what it is.

'Until yesterday morning, I knew neither that cats had cerebra, nor that they could mull things over with them. Cats' brains were a closed book to me, before I opened *The Concise Encyclopaedia of Cats*. I found it in Child's Hill Public Library, while the cat waited outside. When I came out again, the cat looked up at me, so I showed it the book, because, by dint of a cursory flip while the librarian did her stuff, I had by that time discovered that it had a cerebrum and I wanted to keep it abreast of developments. Then I walked home. The cat followed. It's about a mile.

'"Do you have a lot of cats?" the librarian had enquired, stamping.

'"None," I replied. "But one's been following me for three days. I thought I'd try to find out why."

'"It loves you," said the librarian. "They do that, with catpeople."

'"I am not a catperson," I said.

'The librarian smiled a catperson's smile. "You may not *think* you are," she said.

'The cat had picked me up on Monday morning. I was taking my usual shortcut home through Hampstead Cemetery, and I had paused at the mottled headstone of Vitruvius Wyatt (1824–97) to wonder why anyone should be christened Vitruvius, when the cat came out from behind it. It was a predominantly black cat, but with a half-white face – as if Andrew Lloyd Webber, having wisely concluded that his musical bucket could not go twice to the well, had decided to tailor his ambitions to *The Cat of the Opera* – and a white tail.

'I paid it no attention, and strolled on. It strolled after. When I stopped at the tomb of James Clarke, landlord of Jack Straw's Castle, to regret that nobody in 1913 had mustered the facetiousness to chisel *Time, Please!* above his remains, the cat stopped, too. And when I hurried on (for graveyards have a way of suddenly reminding you not to hang about) the cat likewise put boot to throttle. I arrived home, and it stopped at the step; I opened the front door, but it showed no inclination to enter. It was not after food or shelter. What was it after?

'It sat there all day, but whether it vanished with the gloaming or merely because of it, I did not notice. Certainly, it had gone by midnight, when I put out the empty milk bottles; but when I took in the full ones on Tuesday morning, it was back. It did not stir until noon, when I walked a mile to the shops. It sat outside three of them, then it walked back at my heels. I stopped at West Hampstead nick, and went in to ask if anyone had reported a lost cat, but they said they didn't do cats, it's bad enough doing dogs, try sticking a note on the gate, so I came out again, and the cat got off the bonnet of a Panda car and fell back in step. It spent the afternoon outside my front door again, was gone at midnight, and back on Wednesday morning. We walked to the library.

'The encyclopaedia was not the only book we borrowed. We also took out Desmond Morris's *Catwatching* and, God help us, Beverley Nichols's *Cats A–Z*. Useless, the pair of them: Mr Morris has 60 chapters with titles like *Why Do Cats Eat Grass?* and *Why Does a Cat Wag its Tail?* but you will search in vain for *Why Does a Cat Follow You up the Pub?* and Beverley Nichols says F stands for fur. Since he also says the best way to appreciate a cat's fur is to have a candle-lit dinner with it, I saw little point in investigating what he had entered under P. The odds against Beverley and his moggie ever having tied a few on at the Cricklewood Tavern seemed somewhat long.

'It is Thursday morning as I write, the cat is back on the front step, and I do not know what to do next. I had planned to take a walk across Hampstead Heath, but as it is generally full of tattooed blokes with Alsatians and Rottweilers at their heels, I should feel a bit of a . . .

'A bit of a catperson.'

Cats' Tales

When Sidney Denham remarked in *Cats Between Covers* that 'everyone over the age of five in the English-speaking world knows at least two cat stories', he had in his conscious mind such stories of childhood as *Puss in Boots* and *Dick Whittington*. But below the surface of his thought lay a cultural reserve of beliefs about and attitudes to the cat built up over many generations. Yeats, in emphasizing the strange, almost uncanny relationship between the cat running in the grass and the 'pure cold light in the sky' above it, in his poem *The Cat and the Moon*, was giving form to the beliefs held by the Ancient Egyptians many centuries ago. And still, at the end of the rational 20th century, the cat is the subject of all sorts of myths, stories and beliefs.

We might reject the view of the cat held within the religious cultures of the East, but we still think, as Sir Walter Scott once wrote, 'Cats are a mysterious kind of folk. There is more passing in their minds than we are aware of.'

Weather Reports

Tales of the cat's ability to predict, influence and even bring about changes in the weather have long been a part of the myth of the cat in many cultures. The belief that the cat could predict weather changes depended on observations of the cat's actions, great and small, and came to be passed on from one generation to the next as the sayings and proverbs of folklore. Belief in the cat's ability actually to change weather patterns is probably older, stemming from ancient religious beliefs and practices, particularly from those aimed at increasing the fertility of the land.

Rain-making was believed to be a particularly valuable use for the cat among many peoples. A rain-making ritual in the Indonesian island of Celebes involved fastening a cat into a sedan chair and carrying it round a dried-out field three times. The cat would have water sprayed on it and the people following the chair would chant rain-making words. Ritualized ducking or bathing of cats in water to produce rain was a custom in several parts of south-east Asia, especially Malaya, and in Sumatra black cats were used in rain-making rituals because it was believed the darkness of the cat would influence the sky to darken with rain clouds.

The malevolent side of the cat's rain-making ability manifested itself in the European medieval belief that witches in the form of cats could raise tempests and sink ships. Scotland is the home of numerous tales of witches' cats raising tempests. Among the best-known is the story of the Spanish king who sent a warship to Mull to avenge the murder of his daughter by a Scottish witch. The witches of Mull transformed themselves into cats and scattered themselves among the shrouds of the Spanish ship, intending to sink it. But the Spanish captain's own magic arts prevailed against them and they were forced to call upon their Highland queen. Taking the form of a huge black cat, she perched herself at the top of the ship's mast, from where she had only to begin chanting one of her spells to make the ship and all hands sink like a stone.

The witch did not always have to turn into a cat to create storms. Often the witch, retaining her own shape, would use a cat as part of the ritual. Stories of such happenings even found their way into courts of law, most notably in the trial, in which King James VI of Scotland took a personal interest, of Agnes Sampson and the Berwick Witches. She was accused of attempting to shipwreck and drown the king and his wife, Anne of Denmark, as they returned home from Denmark in 1590. During her trial, Agnes Sampson described how a cat was christened, had parts of dead men bound to its limbs, and was then dropped into the midst of the sea off the town of Leith. Sure enough, the greatest tempest ever seen off Leith followed, overwhelming a ship laden with riches for James's new Queen. Agnes Sampson was hanged and her body burned.

Some feline actions to look for when attempting to predict the weather are:

A cat sneezing suddenly or scratching furiously behind its ear, which used to be taken as a sign that rain was on the way.

According to Edward Topsell, 'some observe that if she put hir feete beyond the crowne of her head, that it is a presage of raine'.

Another version of this, collected with other weatherlore in the 19th century, was that 'when cats wipe their jaws with their feet, it is a sign of rain, especially when they put their paws over their ears when wiping'.

A cat sleeping with its paws over its nose could be a sign of gales to come.

For the Chinese, a 'winking cat', sleeping among peonies, would wink an eye at the approach of rain.

And a poetic observation from Jonathan Swift:

> 'Careful observers may foretell the hour
> (By sure prognostics) when to dread a shower,
> While rain depends, the pensive cat gives o'er
> Her frolics and pursues her tail no more.'

A cat washing vigorously behind its ears is a sign of heavy rain, with the wind coming from the direction the cat is facing.

A cat lying curled up with the flat part of the top of its head on the ground is another sign of rain . . . 'Cat on its brain, It's going to rain.'

A cat sitting with its back to the fire or against a warm place could mean frost on the way.

In the nautical world, many beliefs and superstitions surrounded the cat's supposed influence on the weather.

Tortoiseshell cats, in particular, used always to be welcomed on board ship, since they were thought to bring good fortune to it and protect the crew from harm. Both the Scots and the Japanese believed that tortoiseshell cats were particularly good at forecasting storms. Japanese sailors would go so far as to hoist their tortoiseshell cats to the top of the ship's mast so that it could scare off storm devils.

A ship's cat of any colour, if it were being particularly playful and running up and down the deck, was generally taken as a sign of storms to come. The 1849 edition of John Brand's *Observations on Popular Antiquities* reports: 'Sailors, I am informed on the authority of a naval officer, have a great dislike to see the cat, on board ship, unusually playful and frolicsome: such an event, they consider, prognosticates a storm: and they have a saying on these occasions that "the cat has a gale of wind in her tail".'

Brand also notes that the common sailors accounted it very unlucky to throw a cat overboard, or to drown one at sea; Greek sailors had believed for centuries that to do such a thing would certainly cause a storm to arise.

Even when on land, cats could adversely influence sailors' lives. Shutting up a cat, or putting it under a pot, could cause adverse winds and even storms to arise. 'The sailors declare there is somebody on shore keeping a black cat under a tub, which it stands to reason must keep us in harbour,' Charles Darwin noted in his diary while waiting for a favourable wind to get HMS *Beagle* out of harbour.

Among fishermen of the Scottish islands, some words, including 'cat', were taboo and must not be uttered when lines were being set.

Ghosts And Apparitions

The belief in an afterlife for cats is an old one. The Ancient Egyptians, sending their mummified cats into the afterlife, sent

mummified mice with them to provide sustenance on the journey. A long-held belief of Germanic folklore, which directs that if you kill a cat, you must bury it by the light of the moon, or it will come back to haunt you, is still repeated by descendants of German immigrants in the United States today.

As recently as mid-1990, the Rev Matthias Pöhland from Greiz in East Germany was suspended by the Evangelical and Lutheran Church of Thuringia because he had baptized cats to satisfy their owners. The Rev Pöhland justified his feline baptisms by claiming that baptism is the expression of hope for the redemption of non-human life.

For many people, an afterlife for cats is not just something to be hoped for; there are enough well-attested cases of cat ghosts, surely, to convince even the most sceptical that cats do have souls and, therefore, an afterlife.

In 1913, a well-known British researcher in the paranormal, Elliott O'Donnell, published a book devoted entirely to supernatural animal manifestations. In *Animal Ghosts*, he wrote that 'the most common forms of animal phenomena seen in haunted houses are undoubtedly those of cats', and cited one street in Whitechapel, in London's East End, where no fewer than four houses were haunted by cats. He gave two reasons to account for this.

First was the fact that cats, 'more than any other animals that live in houses, meet with sudden and unnatural ends, especially in the poorer districts, where the doctrine of kindness to animals has not yet made itself thoroughly felt'; and, second, was the fact that 'from endless experiments made in haunted houses, I have proved to my own satisfaction, at least, that the [living] cat acts as a thoroughly reliable psychic barometer. The dog is sometimes unaware of the proximity of the Unknown. When the ghost materializes or in some other way demonstrates its advent, the dog, occasionally, is wholly undisturbed – the cat never. I have never yet had a cat with me that has not shown the most obvious signs of terror and uneasiness both before and during a supernatural manifestation.'

Elliott O'Donnell's argument that cats have a spirit came to a resounding climax in words which have a startlingly modern ring: 'Is it not contrary to reason, instinct, and observation to suppose that the many thoroughly material and grossly minded people – people whose whole beings are steeped in money worship – we see around us every day should have spirits, and that pretty, unrefined and artistic-looking cats, whose occult powers place them in the very closest connection with the superphysical, should not?'

The first case of a cat haunting a house which Elliott O'Donnell included in his book must have been one of the very first to come his way, for it was told him by the classics mistress at his preparatory school. The house in question, the Old Manor House at a place called Oxenby, in England, was later visited by O'Donnell and his wife, who wrote a note in *Animal Ghosts* attesting to the truth of her husband's account.

The story of the cat ghost at the Manor House certainly had all the right ingredients: a very old house, dating back at least to the reign of Edward VI, built of grey stone and gloomy of aspect, with 'the device of a cat, constructed out of black shingles and having white shingles for the eyes' on the centre of its frowning and menacing front, and with one dark-shadowed wing unfurnished and shut up. Into this house moved the girl who was to become O'Donnell's classics teacher. Naturally, the little girl was drawn to the closed-up wing of the house, where she several times encountered fearful, indefinite shapes and heard frightful sounds coming out of the gloomy recesses of damp, dusty rooms. Once, she was confronted by a male figure of truly hideous aspect 'clad in some sort of tight-fitting, fantastic garment'.

On another visit to the old wing, the girl saw a door opening, apparently of its own accord. 'Bit by bit, inch by inch, I watched the gap slowly widen. At last, just as I felt I must either go mad or die,

something appeared – and, to my utter astonishment, it was a big black cat! Limping painfully, it came towards me with a curious gliding motion, and I perceived with a thrill of horror that it had been very cruelly maltreated. One of its eyes looked as if it had been gouged out – its ears were lacerated, whilst the paw of one of its hind legs had either been torn or hacked off . . . It made a feeble and pathetic effort to reach me and rub itself against my legs . . . but in so doing it fell down, and uttering a half purr, half gurgle, vanished, seeming to sink through the hard oak boards.'

That evening, the girl's youngest brother met with an accident in the barn, and died.

It was two years before the girl again ventured into the old wing. When she did, she saw the big black cat, stretched out in the last convulsions of death, maimed and bleeding. At noon that day, the girl's mother had an apoplectic seizure and died at midnight.

After this, four years were to pass before the girl went back into the old wing, sent there on an errand by her father. Having carried out her task, she was leaving the wing, 'when a dark shadow fell athwart the threshold of the door, and I saw the cat'. That evening, the girl's father, who had long suffered from heart disease, dropped dead in the fields. After that, the girl and her remaining family left the Manor House, never to go back.

When O'Donnell visited the house he heard that the present occupants of the house, and their servants and many visitors, had all seen the ghastly phantasms of the old man in medieval dress and the bleeding and wounded cat in the old wing, which was eventually locked up, though not before excavations in its cellars and passages had uncovered the skeletons of three men, two women and a boy, all of which were given a decent burial in the nearby churchyard. Some delving into local traditions had also unearthed tales of criminal doings, including the murder of a boy heir to the property and his substitution by the bastard son of the heir's guardian. Among other horrible deeds attributed to the murderer and his son was the mutilation and destruction of the boy heir's pet cat.

That cat ghosts do not just live in gloomy old country houses, to be seen only by impressionable young girls, was made clear by the title of another story in O'Donnell's collection: 'The Headless Cat of No. —, Lower Seedley Road, Seedley, Manchester'.

This time, the story was told to O'Donnell by Mr Robert Dane, a solicitor who, 'like the generality of solicitors', described himself as 'stodgy and unimaginative, whilst my wife is the most practical and matter-of-fact little woman you would hope to meet in a day's march'. Moreover, this respectable couple lived with their children and servants in a house which was 'airy and light – no dark corners, no sinister staircases – and equipped throughout with all modern conveniences'.

Despite this, the family had been living in the house in Lower Seedley Road for only four months when horrid things began to manifest themselves, beginning with just an eye – a large, red and lurid eye – staring at Mr Dane and his brother-in-law from the fire grate. Then came the dreadful sounds of a cat fighting for its life amidst a pack of dogs, with screeches, growls and snarls waking the household, but with nothing to be seen when Mr Dane investigated them. Then the cook handed in her notice and left within the day, having been woken in her bed by scratchings and screeches in her room, followed by something heavy springing on to the bed and landing on top of her.

The climax to all this came one Sunday morning when Mrs Dane was alone, writing a letter in the drawing room. Thinking she could hear a cat mewing under the sofa, she went to investigate, but nothing was to be seen, so she returned to her desk. Suddenly the mewing got louder, there came the sound of some creature crawling out from under the sofa, then something which Mrs Dane still could not see sprang on to her lap and dug its claws into her knees. Then Mrs Dane saw it – a large, tabby cat without a head, its neck terminating in a mangled stump. Mrs Dane fainted. She came to in hysterics, her children and their nurse beside her, but no cat.

Mr and Mrs Dane moved out of the house within ten days of Mrs Dane's terrible experience, but not before Mr Dane was also confronted by the hideous, headless cat, which tried to spring on to his shoulders on the very day they moved out.

Once safely out of the house, Mr Dane began a few enquiries of his own and eventually discovered that about 12 years prior to their residence, the house had been occupied by a couple with a son whom they spoiled outrageously, to the extent of encouraging him in acts of cruelty. Once, they had brought a stray cat into the house, especially for the boy's fox terrier to worry. After being appallingly mangled by the dog, the cat was eventually destroyed by the boy.

Mr Dane found this sad story a very feasible explanation for the hauntings. 'If human tragedies are re-enacted by ghosts, why not animal tragedies, too? It is absurd to suppose man has the monopoly of soul or spirit.'

Borley Rectory, built in 1863 near the 12th-century church at Borley, two-and-a-half miles from Sudbury in Suffolk, was destroyed by fire in 1939. This outwardly ordinary-looking Victorian house was once described as 'the most haunted house in England'. The man who so described the house, a writer and investigator into the paranormal called Harry Price, published two books about Borley Rectory, describing the strange and inexplicable things seen and heard in the house and its surroundings almost from the time it was built until after its burnt-out shell was razed. Harry Price was accused by some investigators into the Borley story of being duplicitous and deceiving in his efforts to promote Borley as the supreme example of the paranormal in Britain; but in 1969 he was vindicated in a detailed report by a member of the Society for Psychical Research.

The story of Borley continues to fascinate people, not least because it has proved impossible to provide rational explanations for all the strange things that happened in the house, or, on the other hand, to find any events in the past history of the land on which the rectory was built to account for the ghostly presences, including a nun, a monk, a man who seemed to be a groom, and a coach-and-horses, seen so often by so many people, and the tappings, ringing bells and echoing footsteps heard over and over again.

A detailed evaluation of the Borley story, *The Ghosts of Borley*, by Paul Tabori and Peter Underwood, was published in 1973; it is from this book that the details of the Borley cat ghost come.

A huge, spectral black cat appeared among the ghosts of Borley Rectory rather late in the Rectory's existence. There had long been a cats' cemetery in the Rectory garden, where the pets of the first occupants of the Rectory, the Rev Henry E. D. Bull and his large family, had been carefully buried, and it was possible that their last resting place impinged on the burial place of some victims of the Great Plague of 1665, believed to have been buried in the ground that became the Rectory garden. The cats' cemetery was itself disturbed by persons unknown, but was that enough to account for the huge black cat which, on at least two occasions, shot between the legs of men standing outside the ruins of the Rectory, and bolted into the house, never coming out again? Enquiries among people living near the Rectory produced no black cats from among them – only stories that many people in the garden at night had seen a cat run rapidly into the house and never come out again.

Ten years after the fire which destroyed Borley Rectory, the spectral cat was still showing itself at Borley. Now it had moved its appearances to the cottage in the garden that was all that was left of the Rectory buildings. The cottage was inhabited by a couple who had had several cats of their own, so the first reappearance of the strange cat – scratching at the bedclothes at night – did not immediately make them think of ghosts; they thought it was one of their own cats in the bedroom, until a search of the room and the landing outside made them realize it could not have been.

Some time later, a 'mysterious furry form' was seen chasing Fred, one of the family's cats, under their car. This time, the cat was not huge and black, but thin, scraggy and a grey-white in colour. When the terrified Fred shot back out from under the car and up a tree, the second cat did not; in fact, there was no sign of it.

Later, a visitor to the cottage was in the bathroom when he saw a distinctly feline shape moving against the bath; realizing it did not look like either of the family's cats, the visitor turned from the basin to get a better look. There was nothing there. His later description of the cat shape he had seen tallied exactly with that of the 'furry form' which had so terrified Fred not long before.

The phantom cat's last appearance in the Borley cottage was a vocal one. One evening, when Fred was sleeping peacefully on the sofa beside his owner, and the family's other cat, Holly, was out in the garden, a terrible feline squeal, as from a cat whose tail had just been trodden on heavily, was heard from inside the house, seemingly on the landing. There was no cat to be seen in the house – apart from Fred, lying peacefully on the sofa.

After this, the family left the cottage, taking Fred and Holly with them, and spectral cats were seen no more around Borley.

For some light relief, of an admittedly macabre kind, we can turn to Ferryford, near Trenton, New Jersey, in the USA, in 1921. This tale of two ghosts on the loose was reported in the London newspaper, the *Weekly Despatch*, which told its readers on 3 April that the inhabitants of Ferryford had become so unnerved by the sight of a spectral figure which was stalking their town nightly, accompanied by a large white cat, that they were leaving in large numbers.

The spectre was said to be that of one John Koch, an automobile repair shop owner who six months previously had quarrelled with one of his staff and shot him and then committed suicide. The newspaper reported that Koch, with an enormous white cat, was said to have entered the living-room of the cottage where he had lived, spreading panic among his widow and her friends before whistling to his cat and leaving. He repeated this performance twice in the following week.

Eventually, a party of people, headed by the local policeman, surrounded Koch's former cottage. Among them was a man from whom Koch had borrowed money the day before his death, and a dog, the latter being of the party so that it could investigate the cat.

Shortly after midnight, a crash was heard from the cottage, and a portrait of Koch's mother-in-law was found to have fallen to the floor. Then the onlookers heard a hollow laugh, and Koch appeared at a window, surrounded by a faint blue mist. Behind him in the garden, a large white cat with long whiskers sat in a pear tree. The dog let out a loud bark and sprang at the cat, but it passed right through the cat, its jaws snapping at the empty air. The dog's barks now turned to howls and it fled.

The rest of the party threw anything to hand at Koch, who merely smiled sardonically, called the cat and faded away.

The details of this story are so delightful, that one would be sorry to have to disbelieve it. There would seem to have been no follow-up story in the *Weekly Despatch* to give any final note on the tale.

And now for a happy ghost story involving two cats, living perhaps 300 years apart, but still in tune with each other, and bearing out Elliott O'Donnell's belief in the cat's ability to be a reliable psychic barometer – though not his belief that living cats are always terrified by psychic manifestations. The story, recounted by Hilary Stainer Rice in her book, *Ghosts of the Chilterns and Thames Valley*, was told to her by a retired RAF Wing Commander who, with his wife, bought a cottage dating from about 1650 in Whitchurch in Buckinghamshire, England.

They moved in, with their longhaired tabby, Tootsie, in the summer of 1970. Tootsie was an affectionate, docile cat, who seldom purred, yet the evening they drove up to the cottage for the first time, she put her paws up on the car's windowsill and, peering at the cottage in the darkness, began to purr loudly. When she walked into the cottage it was obvious that she was immediately at home in happy contentment.

Soon, the Wing Commander's wife began to see a shadowy black cat in the cottage. She saw it walk, tail erect, through the dining-room and out through a wall where there had once been a front door into the cottage. After his wife had seen the black cat at regular intervals for some time, the Wing Commander began to see it, too. It always came in the back door of the cottage, through the dining-room and went out through the front wall.

Once some visitors from Canada, who had not been told of the cottage's ghost cat, saw it walk in the back door and on another occasion a cat-hating miniature dachshund on a visit suddenly erupted in fierce growls and shot across the room to the wall at the point where the ghost cat always walked through.

The ghostly black cat continued to trot through the cottage, tail erect, at intervals until 1977 when Tootsie became ill and had to be put to sleep. Although the Wing Commander and his wife obtained another cat and continued to live in the cottage until 1981 they never again saw the little black cat walk, tail up, through their house.

'I have no doubt there was some inexplicable affiliation between Tootsie and the black ghost cat always with its tail erect!' wrote the Wing Commander.

If the RAF man's cat was a clairvoyant, it was obviously a happy one, pleased to be sharing its new home with a cat that could walk through walls. This is unusual in the general run of stories about cats who have displayed an awareness of a 'presence' invisible to the ordinary senses. Maurice Howey, in *The Cat in the Mysteries of Religion and Magic*, repeats an incident investigated by the Society for Psychical Research in the 1880s, in which both the cat and its owner experienced the supernatural – and were both very unhappy to have done so.

On this occasion, the ghost was not that of a dead cat, but of a dead woman. The strange and horrible event occurred in Boulogne-sur-Mer, France, in 1845, where the woman who described the incident was staying with her mother and their cat. The woman was sitting in a room, brightly lit by a large fire, with the much-loved cat – 'the illustrious Lady Catherine' – on her knee. Both were relaxed and happy, the cat purring contentedly.

Gradually, the woman became aware that her cat's equanimity was becoming disturbed, she had stopped purring and was becoming ever more restless and obviously uneasy. Suddenly, the cat leapt to her feet, spitting with fury, her back arched and her fur standing on end.

'The change in her position obliged me to raise my head,' the woman recalled later, 'and, on looking up, to my inexpressible horror, I then perceived [that] a little, hideous, wrinkled old hag occupied Mamma's chair . . . Her eyes, piercingly fierce and shining with an overpowering lustre, were glaring at me . . .' The woman was rooted to her own chair, paralysed with fright.

Not so the cat. She was in violent movement, leaping over the furniture, hurling herself at the door in a vain attempt to get out of that dreadful room. Eventually, the woman got her breath back and managed to scream loudly, bringing her mother into the room. The cat shot out of the door and the old hag – had gone!

'I had walled the monster up within the tomb!' – the climactic moment from Edgar Allan Poe's sinister tale of suspense, The Black Cat *, illustrated in fearsome detail by Harry Clarke.*

It was a long time before the cat had calmed down sufficiently to allow itself to be comforted, and we are not told if it ever went back into the sitting-room again, or if the old woman was seen in it on other occasions. Perhaps mother, daughter and cat moved out of the house with all possible speed. If they did not move at once, they must surely have done so when, some time later, they discovered that a former owner of the house – an old lady – had hanged herself in the very room in which the woman and her cat were sitting so peacefully on that never-to-be-forgotten winter night in 1845.

So far, all our stories of ghostly cats have involved houses, most of them either long since destroyed, of unknown address, or private property. Two ghost stories, one in Ireland and one in France, are centred on buildings which still exist and may be visited.

The Irish cat ghost was documented by John J. Dunne in *Haunted Ireland: Her Romantic and Mysterious Ghosts*. The ghost, a ferocious black cat, was long the subject of many stories around the small town of Killakee, in the south of County Dublin. Its main stalking area was the land around a hunting lodge built by William Connolly, a Speaker of the Irish House of Commons, on the slopes of Mount Pelier, the adjoining estate of Lord Massey, and several other old buildings in the district. There were many stories of the ghostly cat having been encountered in the lonely lanes of the area.

The memory of the ghost cat lingered longest on the Massey estate, despite the fact that the mansion was in ruins and the cat carvings on the stonework of the old house had long since been destroyed.

Eventually, part of the Massey estate's Dower House was converted into an arts centre. Almost from the time they moved into the new centre, the owners noticed many weird things happening in the house, as if a poltergeist were on the loose: furniture would be moved and broken and crockery smashed, and on one occasion in 1970 the coffee bar was wrecked, an incident which was reported in the Dublin newspapers. A year or so before the wrecking of the coffee bar, a ghost had been exorcized in the house, after visitors had seen standing in a doorway a three-foot-high crippled man who had turned into a cat before their very eyes.

Apparently, the newspaper stories were seen by an Austrian priest visiting Ireland at the time. Experienced in such phenomena, he visited the arts centre, discovered that a seance had been held in the house at some recent time, and came to the conclusion that the 'poltergeist entity' of the house had been disturbed – hence all the strange happenings. To help everything settle down again, the owners of the arts centre were advised to remove from above the door of the gallery the figure of a cat which had been taken from the headstone of a crippled boy who had lived in the house 150 years before.

The Castle of Combourg in Brittany, south of Dol de Bretagne, is a place of literary pilgrimage in France, because of its associations with the writer François-René de Chateaubriand. It is also a place of interest to seekers after feline ghosts and psychic phenomena because it is one of only a few buildings open to the public where cat ghosts have been reported.

The grim and gloomy-looking castle was built in the 11th century and has among its several great towers one called the Tour du

Chat – the Cat Tower. This tower was long thought to be haunted by the ghost of a former Count of Combourg – or, at least, a part of him. The Count had a wooden leg and is said to have left behind him after his death a wraith of his wooden leg, which was seen on numerous occasions perambulating the Grand Staircase of the Cat Tower, accompanied by a spectral black cat. The *Michelin Guide to Brittany* rejects the ghostly wooden leg and notes that it is the former Count of Combourg himself who is said to haunt the Cat Tower in the shape of a black cat.

The story of the black cat ghost was certainly known to the young Chateaubriand when he lived in the castle, which was owned by his father, in the mid-18th century. Chateaubriand was given a lonely room in the tower, where the boy lay awake at night anxiously watching and listening for the ghostly cat. 'The owls fluttering against the window and the wind rattling the door and howling in the corridors made him shiver,' remarks The *Michelin Guide*. 'It was there that the dreamy and melancholy soul of the writer was formed, or perhaps confirmed.'

Visitors to the castle today may see Chateaubriand's room and the former castle archive room in the tower, which have been turned into a museum containing souvenirs of the writer's life including the bed in which he died in Paris. The *Michelin Guide* recommends visitors to look at the very fine view from the Cat Tower but offers no hints as to where the ghostly cat might be observed.

Perhaps it has long since gone. It certainly does not seem to have given Chateaubriand a dislike of cats. On the contrary, 'I love in the cat that independent and almost ungrateful temper which prevents him from attaching himself to anyone,' he once wrote 'When you caress him, he stretches himself out and arches his back, indeed, but that is caused by physical pleasure, not, as in the case of the dog, by a silly satisfaction in loving and being faithful to a master who returns thanks in kicks . . .'

There are many stories of cats – nearly always black cats – appearing again in houses where they had lived, but where their lives ended abruptly and, often, in unhappy circumstances.

Grace McHattie, former editor of *Cat World* magazine, has told how she frequently saw a black cat in the garden of a house she and her family had just moved into. Every time she looked for the cat, it had disappeared. None of the neighbours had a black cat, nor was one known to be in the area. One day, someone told her that there had been a black cat living in the house many years before. It had not been well treated, and had been left to have litter after litter of kittens under a nearby railway bridge. When Ms McHattie's own cats moved in, the black cat stopped appearing in the garden and was not seen again.

Another cat ghost in Hilary Stainer Rice's collection, *Ghosts of the Chilterns and Thames Valley*, was also a black one, seen by several members of a Buckinghamshire family in their house. They had no cat of their own, so their frequent sightings of this handsome fluffy feline could not have been a matter of mistaken identity. So real did the ghost cat seem that an aunt, carrying a loaded tea tray into the sitting room, dropped it because, she said, 'that cat' had caused her to trip.

Eventually, the family discovered that the previous owner of the house had had several dogs and a number of cats, including a beautiful black Persian. One day, one of the dogs, an Alsatian, had killed the Persian cat in the sitting room – the room in which the ghostly fluffy cat was always seen.

That ghost cats choose for themselves whom they will appear to seems to be borne out by a true story told to the writer, Stella Whitelaw, which she included in her book *Cats' Tales: A Treasury*.

Once again, the people who saw the black cat had just moved into the old, red-brick house. When the mother first saw the cat walk into her larder, she thought it was real, and followed it to chase it outside. There was no cat in the larder, and nowhere it could have hidden or escaped through.

The mother saw the black cat with the slanting amber eyes almost daily for several weeks, but her husband never saw it. One day, one of their small daughters also saw the cat, and became so used to it, she christened it 'Spooky'. Then the second daughter felt the cat sitting on her legs in bed one morning, and stretched out, quite naturally, to stroke the cat, which, of course, wasn't there.

A year after the family moved into the house, a son was born, and the family also acquired a cat of their own. Not long after, the girls found the body of a dead cat. It looked as if it had been squashed by a piece of old machinery, for the obviously long-dead body was underneath it. The cat was buried in the back yard, the girls said prayers over it, and everyone hoped that if this had been Spooky, he would be at peace now.

Spooky did occasionally visit over the years, never being seen by the husband or the son of the family – or, apparently, by the family cat, of which there were several over the years. Then, when the son was 15, the family cat encountered 'something' in the kitchen which turned it into a very nervous cat indeed. It shot out of the kitchen, hair on end, and hid itself in the son's bedroom, refusing to come out. The son investigated, but found nothing. For a long time the cat refused to go into the kitchen at all, then when eventually it did, it avoided all contact with the floor and walked on the furniture to get from one side of the room to the other. During this time none of the women of the house saw their old ghost, Spooky. Could the house have acquired another ghost?

Soon, the mother had another little girl in the house – her first granddaughter, who even at two years old seemed to be seeing a cat about the house that other people could not see . . .

Ghost cats sitting on posts have been seen in widely distant parts of England. A phantom cat with huge eyes 'like saucers' has been seen at intervals over many years sitting on a stone gatepost near Morwenstow in Cornwall. The most recent sighting of this cat to be noted was in December 1957.

Up north, near Congleton, in Cheshire, the 'cat on a post' was, apparently, last seen on two occasions, only days apart, early this century. It had been known to local people for some 40 or more years before this, however.

When last seen, the handsome, white Congleton ghost cat wafted a friendly air towards the two women – sensible ladies both – who saw it sitting on the post by the roadside, but when one of the women approached it, thinking it a perfectly ordinary cat, it jumped into the air and disappeared – into thin air, since there were no bushes, hedges or trees for it to leap into from the post.

Later, the women were told it must have been the local ghost cat seen several times by local people. One elderly lady even remembered the cat when it had been alive, the much-loved pet of a local woman, who was the housekeeper at a house which had once been an abbey. One day, the cat disappeared and the housekeeper was afraid that it had been killed by dogs roaming loose in the area. When she heard a familiar scratching at an outside door, she was much relieved to think that the cat had returned home safely after all, and hurried to open the door. Sure enough, there was her beloved pet sitting calmly on the doormat. But, though she called and coaxed, the cat would not enter the house. Then the cat disappeared – not suddenly, as it was to do for the two women so many years later, but gradually, bit by bit, rather like the Cheshire Cat in *Alice in Wonderland*.

The white cat reappeared on numerous occasions after this, being seen by its former owner and friends and visitors to the abbey. By the turn of the century, it was being seen in places some way from the abbey and by people with no connection with Congleton. Perhaps because its loving owner was no longer there, the cat felt no further need to remain there itself.

Behind Every Author . . .

. . . there's a cat. Well, not every author, perhaps, but it is true that behind the scenes in the creating of many books, cats have been working away, exerting their influence and making their presence felt, for good and bad.

Back in the 16th century, when Constanzo Felici of Piobbcio was gathering the material for one of the earliest health food cookery books, *An Essay of Salads* (1565–9), the family cat was being a nuisance. Felici was trying to preserve some fish by hanging it up in the chimney and his cat ate it. On another occasion, as Felici wrote to his friend, the botanist and naturalist Ulisse Aldrovandi, Felici had to send his friend a drawing of the fish he had just described in his letter because 'the moment my back was turned a

This splendid tabby cat, apparently existing happily with a little brown mouse, comes from a manuscript in the collection of the great 16th-century naturalist and botanist Ulisse Aldrovandi. The cat may be the one who, on more than one occasion, upset the work of Aldrovandi's correspondent and fellow naturalist, Constanzo Felici.

passing cat dragged it off the table and ruined its head', making it not worth preserving and sending on to the naturalist. Still in the Aldrovandi archive in the University Library at Bologna is a splendid picture of a cat with a wondrously striped tail, and a mouse sitting by his front paws; both animals are surrounded by paintings of cherries, a fig, pears and other foods. It is agreeable to think that this might be Felici's fish-stealing cat.

When Daniel Defoe took Alexander Selkirk as the model for the hero of *Robinson Crusoe*, he used the Scotsman just as the jumping-off point for his story, ignoring those aspects of Selkirk's five-year sojourn on the island of Más á Tierra which did not suit his purpose – including the cats. Cats? No Man Friday? Not according to Woodes Rogers, the buccaneer who eventually picked up Selkirk from the island in the Pacific 400 miles west of Chile. Here is part of Rogers' account of Selkirk on the island:

'He had with him his clothes and bedding, with a firelock, some powder, bullets and tobacco, a hatchet, a knife, a kettle, a Bible, some practical pieces, and his mathematical instruments and books. He built two huts with pimento trees, covered them with long grass, and lined them with the skins of goats, which he killed with his gun as he wanted, so long as his powder lasted . . . When his powder failed, he took them by speed of feet . . . He was at first much pestered with cats and rats, that bred in great numbers from some of the species which had got ashore from ships that put in there to wood and water. The rats gnawed at his feet and clothes while asleep, which obliged him to cherish the cats with his goats' flesh, by which many of them became so tame that they would lie about him in hundreds, and soon delivered him from the rats. He likewise tamed some kids, and to divert himself would . . . sing and dance with them and his cats.'

The Rev James Woodforde, whose diaries, published as *Diary of a Country Parson* in five volumes in the 1920s, turned him into one of the 18th century's best-known literary parsons, kept a cat in his rectory at Weston Longville in Norfolk. Parson Woodforde would seem to have been interested in practical medicine – he records in his diary dosing his household against the Whirligig-ousticon (malaria) and other agues – and was not averse to using old-fashioned remedies, including his cat's tail. 'The Stiony [sty] on my right Eye-lid still swelled and inflamed very much,' he noted in his diary in March 1791. 'As it is commonly said that the Eye-lid being rubbed by the tail of a black Cat would do it much good if not entirely cure it, and having a black Cat, a little before dinner I made a trial of it, and very soon after dinner I found my Eye-lid much abated of the swelling and almost free from Pain. I cannot therefore but conclude it to be of the greatest service to a Stiony on the Eye-lid. Any other Cat's Tail may have the above effect in all probability – but I did my Eye-lid with my own black Tom Cat's Tail.'

Charles Dickens and his family liked to have cats about them. One of his cats, brought into the household as 'William', had to be rechristened 'Wilhelmina' when she produced kittens. One of Wilhelmina's kittens became Dickens' special cat, which the family called 'The Master's Cat'. Mary, Charles Dickens' daughter, told in her memoirs of her father a story of the novelist's reading being interrupted by the cat: ' "The Master" was reading at a small table; suddenly the candle went out. My father, who was much interested in his book, relighted the candle, stroked the cat, who was looking at him pathetically, he noticed, and continued his reading. A few minutes later, as the light became dim, he looked up just in time to see puss deliberately put out the candle with his paw, and then look appealing at him. This second and unmistakable hint was not disregarded and puss was given the petting he craved.'

T. S. Eliot's cats, of which he had several, all with splendid names, were the inspiration behind several of the cats in *Old Possum's Book of Practical Cats*. Perhaps they were also the models for Eliot's own design for the book's cover, which was a drawing of cats climbing a ladder. The original drawings for the front and rear covers of the book were recently sold at auction in London for several thousand pounds. While it was quite a respectable sum for drawings by T. S. Eliot to have achieved, it is insignificant indeed when compared to the royalties *Old Possum's Book of Practical Cats* earns from the musical *Cats*, for which the book was the literary basis: these royalties were believed to be benefiting the Eliot estate by some £2 million annually at the end of the 1980s.

At his house in Havana, Cuba, where he lived towards the end of his life, Ernest Hemingway had 30 cats. Hemingway once said that 'a cat has absolute emotional honesty', and his own love for them provides the inspiration for one of his finest pieces of writing about animals, in the central 'Cuba' section of his last novel, *Islands in the Stream*. The novel concerns the life of an artist, Thomas Hudson, who is also, in typical Hemingway style, a fighter, a big game fish-

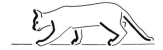

erman and lover of many women. Hudson is also a catperson, and in a superb, 20-page-long section of the book, Hemingway describes Hudson's cats and his relationship with them in a way that makes it clear that Hemingway is describing his own cats, writing down the things he has noticed about them, even to telling about the ones that 'were very odd about catnip' and the ones that would never touch it. And the names of Hudson's cats – were they also the names of Hemingway's cats? There was big, black and white Boise and his son Goats; and there were Willy, Friendless's Brother, Littless, Furhouse, Taskforce, Uncle Woolfie, 'who was as stupid as he was beautiful', and Princessa, the grandmother of all the cats and 'intelligent, delicate, high-principled, aristocratic, and most loving' – when she was not on heat, when she became most wanton.

Alice Thomas Ellis is a writer who has always had cats about her, and writes them into her novels. In *The 27th Kingdom*, the action revolves round a longhaired white cat called Focus, a cat 'with a foolish face' who likes swimming in the sea. Perhaps there is a touch of the Turkish Van about Focus!

Among naturalist Desmond Morris's numerous best-selling books, two of the most popular have been *Catwatching* and *Catlore*. He says himself that the books were inspired by his big, black cat, Jambo, a lovely female cat who works with Morris in his studio/library in Oxford. Jambo came into the Morris family's life when they returned from a trip to Africa to find her up an apple tree in the garden. Jambo's one eccentricity: she very much dislikes being picked up.

Postcards From Hollywood

Cats have played many parts on the screen. Notes from recent gossip columns and elsewhere have contained a few surprises.

Carlo Rimbaldi, the Hollywood designer who conceived ET, has confessed that he got the Extra-Terrestrial's frontal aspect from oriental cats. But the animator Richard Williams, also involved in creating ET, says that the lovable little creature has Einstein's eyes, because Steven Spielberg wanted ET to be an amalgam of Einstein, Hemingway and Don Pasos, and the Einstein eyes were as near as Williams could get. At least it explains why ET's oriental-cat frontal aspect does not look all that close to the lovely Siamese or Burmese cat.

'Kitty kasting kalls' – several of them – had to be held to find a lookalike for Polar Bear, the real-life cat in Cleveland Amory's books *The Cat Who Came for Christmas* and *The Cat and the Curmudgeon*. Mr Amory revealed in the latter book that the auditions took place because a movie is planned on the best-selling cat's life.

One-hundred-and-fifty cats, mostly strays from Brussels, had parts in a feature-length movie version of Shakespeare's *Romeo and Juliet*, first shown at the Venice Film Festival in 1990. The film took nearly two years to make and involved 350 hours of filming and 4000 hours of editing.

Juliet was played by a beautiful angora 'from the cultured Old World' and Romeo, a 'New World alley cat' in this third version of the story, was a smooth-haired grey. A three-legged Siamese was cast as Mercutio, and the only human in the film was John Hurt, playing a Venetian baglady who rescued stray European cats and took them to America. Providing voices for the cat actors were such famous human voices as Maggie Smith, Robert Powell, Vanessa Redgrave and Ben Kingsley.

The film's director was Armando Acosta, an art director for *Lawrence of Arabia* and director of over 200 commercials. His reasons for making this feline *Romeo and Juliet* sounded like pure Hollywood: 'This classic love theme clearly suggests that truth, that the highest love, is beyond the body. So I thought, why not experience this in a cerebral way, through the mind of the mystical feline?' Also in true Hollywood tradition, Mr Acosta fell for his leading lady. Maria, real name of the feline actress who played Juliet, moved in with the director when filming was completed. But so did Romeo and ten other actors from the movie; perhaps Mr Acosta is keeping his acting stable together for another film. *A Winter's Tail*, maybe.

The Tom and Jerry cartoons were each only seven minutes long, but there are enough of them to make into a feature-length film, so Turner Entertainment Company, present owner of MGM, believes. The original cartoons were created by William Hanna and Joseph Barbera for MGM between 1940 and 1967. Fifty years after the first cartoon, called *Puss Gets the Boot*, was made, Joseph Barbera, now 79, is being called out of retirement to be creative consultant on the project. It should be a great movie, especially as both cat and mouse are being given the gift of speech, which they did not have in the cartoons.

If the film is released in France, it should perhaps carry a feline health warning. Not so long ago a family in Nevers, France, were watching a Tom and Jerry cartoon on television. Also watching was the family's cat, a happy, peace-loving individual who had never done anyone any harm. Then came on to the screen one of those frenetic sequences in which Tom chases Jerry: the cat suddenly went berserk and began attacking the family. The family could not calm their pet down, and called the police. When they arrived they found the man of the house holding the cat at bay with a kitchen chair. Even the vet could not calm the poor cat and it had to be destroyed.

Cat Skills

Healing Powers

Chinese folklore once had it that the snuffling of a dog or cat could revive a corpse. This may be the most extreme view of the healing power of cats to be held by superstitious peoples, but it is not unique. The belief that cats *can* heal human sickness has been held in many cultures, perhaps as a subconscious retention of the Ancient Egyptian belief that Bastet, the cat-goddess, had healing powers, especially over poisonous bites and stings on people.

Even that sophisticated Roman, Pliny, considered cats' faeces to have their medicinal uses; mixed with mustard, the faeces were thought to cure ulcers of the head and, mixed with resin and oil of roses, they were useful for uterine ulcers.

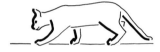

The Japanese used to believe that if a black cat were placed on a sick person's stomach, its fur could cure spasms; a black cat was also thought effective in the cure of melancholia and epilepsy. Many people still believe that a cat's fur can relieve rheumatism, encouraging their pets to sleep beside them at night. This is perhaps the last remnant of the old belief that cat fur was useful for treating both rheumatism and burns; during the Great Fire of London in 1666, dead cats were skinned and their fur placed on badly burned areas of human bodies, acting as an insulation against the air, and thus reducing the pain.

The skin beneath the fur has also been used in treating illness; Dutch people once believed that applying the skin of a newly-dead cat to an inflamed area could cure the inflammation. Other peoples have used cat skin to treat hives and sore throats, or have worn it on the stomach or joints to take away pains.

Won't hurt a bit Mr Jones

The cat's tail (still attached to the living cat) has been used for healing purposes in many places. An old folk remedy for the removal of warts was to rub them with the tail of a tortoiseshell tomcat. Since this remedy was only effective in May and since tortoiseshell male cats are very rare, very few warts must have been cured by this method. Perhaps Huckleberry Finn's cat cure for warts, as outlined in *Tom Sawyer*, would be more effective. Huck said you had to take a cat to a graveyard in the middle of the night, when '. . . Devil follow corpse, cat follow Devil, wart follow cat, that will fetch any wart'.

The tail of a black tomcat was also rubbed over eyes to cure sties until well into the 20th century in England. Generally, it was believed that simply to rub the tail over the affected eye was sufficient treatment, but in some parts of England, more complicated rituals had to be carried out. The eye might have to be brushed with the tail exactly seven times, for instance, or – as in a Northamptonshire belief – the sufferer should, on the first night of the new moon, pull one hair from the tail of a black cat and run the tip nine times over the sty. In Cornwall, you would have to utter a spell while stroking the affected eye with the black cat's tail: 'I poke thee, I don't poke thee, I take the queff that's under the 'ee . . .'

The tails of black cats were also used to cure whitlows: on three successive nights, you had to pass the cat's tail up and down your fingers in a carefully prescribed order.

Sometimes, the cure would involve taking a specified number of drops of blood from the cat's tail and applying them to the affected part of the body, usually in conjunction with some other ritual. Blood obtained from a cat's tail was also believed to be a cure for the 'falling sickness' (epilepsy).

In parts of Ireland it used to be believed that an effective cure for whooping cough could be made from an infusion consisting of nine hairs taken from a black cat's tail, chopped up and soaked in water.

For other illnesses, the healing power of the cat depended on the cat's tail being cut off. It was believed in parts of England that you could keep your whole family in good health if you buried the tail of a black cat under the doorstep. Elsewhere, it was believed that the blood from a cat's tail could cure shingles, either smeared directly on the affected parts, or mixed first with a little fresh milk.

More grisly cures, especially for curing diseases of the eyes, involved killing the cat. Here is Edward Topsell's version of a 17th-century recipe for curing 'the paine and blindnesse in the eye':

'Take the head of a blacke Cat, which hath not a spot of another colour in it, and burne it to pouder . . . ; then take this pouder, and, throughe a quill, blowe it thrice a day into thy eie . . .'

Topsell also suggested that a 'neezing pouder made of the gall of a blacke Cat . . . and the waight of a groate thereof' could help 'Wrynesse of the mouth', while gout might be cured by putting on the affected area fat rendered down from a cat's body.

Now that we are nearing the end of the 20th century we may retain less faith in the old folk remedies, but we have not lost faith in the belief that cats have power to heal human ills. Today, though, the ills may be less physically obvious, the cats are valued for themselves alone, and the belief is based on the evidence of scientifically conducted surveys.

The importance of the human-companion animal bond has been studied by groups of scientists in many parts of the world, with the cat and the dog at the top of the list of desirable animal companions. During the 1980s various studies and surveys were carried out on the relationship between people and pets, and international symposia were held to discuss the findings, thus allowing scientists to discover what cat lovers have always known: having a cat about the house is good for you.

Surveys have shown that people who own pets generally live longer than people who do not. Stroking a cat, or just having one sitting on your lap, can lower blood pressure and heart rates, and a cat's presence may also reduce the levels of many minor problems, including flu, backache and even the common cold.

The Companion Animal Research Group at the University of Cambridge has been carrying out a long-term survey in Britain on the influence of pet ownership on human behaviour, health and well-being and has found that people coming new to the pleasure of owning a cat or dog show a dramatic and positive increase in their mental and physical well-being when compared with non-pet owners. Researchers in the United States have come up with similar findings.

Several studies carried out in the early '80s showed that children with pets tend to have better social skills than their non-pet-owning peers, while pet ownership can also raise morale and increase feelings of cheerfulness and self-esteem among the elderly and lonely. A study by a Los Angeles scientist showed that owning a pet could significantly reduce many of the problems of ill-health and isolation too often associated with old age. Elderly pet owners were likely to have more friends than non-pet owners, and were also more likely to get out and about and join organized groups and clubs.

The benefits of owning a pet can be physical as well as psychological. Scientists have reported a significantly higher survival rate following heart attacks in patients owning a pet. They think that this could be the result of the reduction in stress and the related decrease in blood pressure when handling pets as already noticed by other researchers; even when dogs – who have to be walked by their owners – were taken out of the survey, the beneficial effects remained among owners of other pets, so it was not simply a question of pet owners getting more exercise than non-pet owners.

In the United Kingdom, the benefits of pet contact with the elderly and sick have been recognized officially, with the Royal College of Nursing recently endorsing pet visiting schemes for nursing homes and similar establishments. In 1990, a charity called Pets As Therapy was launched to turn dogs, cats and even a rabbit or two into registered hospital and nursing home visitors.

Coming up in 1992 in Montreal, Canada, is the world's largest-ever conference on the relationship humans have with pets and the environment. Perhaps it will nail forever the old idea that to be healed by a cat we need bits of its fur or drops of blood from its tail; the living, breathing, warm and beautiful cat itself is all we need.

Feline Weather Forecasting

In *The Psychic Powers of Animals*, Bill Schul tells of everyday life among domestic cats in the United States. One of these cats was Felix, from Oklahoma City, who was considered by his owner to be a far more reliable guide to weather than the local TV weather experts. If Felix knew the day was going to be a fine one, he would settle down on his favourite windowsill; if he thought wet and stormy weather was on the way he would take refuge on top of a wardrobe. Felix was never wrong.

It is possible that Felix's apparent ability to detect rain on the way had something to do with his ears. The British scientist, Roger Tabor, has a theory, put forward in *The Wild Life of the Domestic Cat*, that the cat's inner ear and eardrum may be sensitively attuned to detect slight air pressure changes, 'for this is how the vibrational nature of sound makes itself felt. To a lesser extent humidity changes will affect the membrane-free surface.' Which could be why cats rub their ears before it rains: the air pressure changes may be irritating to the sensitive inner ear.

Bill Schul also mentioned in his book the Kansas farmer who realized that when his cat had moved her four kittens, one by one, over a period of days, from their barn to a place some distance away, she had known not only that a tornado was on the way but that the barn was right in its destructive path.

It is this sort of behaviour that has prompted scientists in China, the USA, Chile and the USSR, all countries with earthquake belts, and other countries, to study seriously the behaviour of animals, including cats, during earthquakes. They have come up with some extraordinary stories. They have noticed that entire villagefuls of cats have suddenly left home and taken to the fields and hills some hours before an earthquake has struck the village; they have been told of cats, at home on an apparently calm evening, suddenly trying frantically to get out-of-doors and away from buildings; and they have been told, over and over again, of cats moving their kittens out of buildings or to safer places hours before earthquakes have struck.

In 1970, the government of China began setting up a network of seismographic centres, with a large professional staff and an even larger body of amateurs, all charged with permanently keeping an eye or ear open for abnormal animal behaviour, unexplained changes in the water levels of wells and odd sounds below ground. As a result, when cats and other animals were noticed behaving strangely out of character in the central China city of Haicheng in 1975, a full evacuation of the city was ordered . . . a good 24 hours before a huge earthquake, causing widespread devastation, hit the region.

Scientists still do not know for sure what causes cats to behave as they do before major weather changes, and perhaps they never will. But there are several theories. Dr Helmut Tributsch, a biochemist at the Fritz Haber Institute in Berlin, theorizes that the cat's apparent ability to forecast earthquakes is really an ability to detect the presence of positively charged atoms (ions) which are released in the atmosphere immediately prior to an earthquake. Increased electrical activity in the atmosphere before an earthquake is a well-documented phenomenon. Many humans are sensitive enough to this to feel 'headachy', but cats may suffer pronounced changes in mood and behaviour because of changes in the chemistry of their brains and nervous systems. One of these changes, Dr Tributsch thinks, may be an increase in the production of a chemical messenger called serotonin.

Another scientist, Dr Ernst Kilian, a native of another earthquake-prone country, Chile, has been gathering information about animals and earthquakes for more than 30 years. He believes that cats are able to detect the tiny tremors in the earth's crust which precede major earthquakes. He thinks it is possible that pre-quake tremors have a unique pattern which cats and other animals can detect.

This is a theory held by other scientists in America and elsewhere, which is itself based on another theory – that the relationship between hearing and touch can be very close in animals, so that a cat can 'hear' sounds through the soles of its feet, thus making it particularly sensitive to 'advance warning' tremors.

Testing Your Cat's I.Q.

There are, apparently, people who worry that their cat(s) may not be as bright as other people's or who are unable to decide whether their cats are wonderfully intelligent or beautiful but dim.

For such people, animal behaviourists and others have, from time to time, come up with I.Q. tests devised especially for cats. One of the most recent series of tests is called *The Original Cat I.Q. Test* by Melissa Miller, due to be published in 1992. The test covers four areas – audio skills, visual skills, social skills and domestic skills – and includes a series of questions and propositions with a), b) and c) answers, scoring three, two and one points respectively. Depending on the number of points scored, cats may be graded 'possibly brighter than you are', 'intelligent', 'average' or 'blissfully ignorant'.

Here is a selection of tests from all four parts of *The Original Cat I.Q. Test*. In most cases, the cat being tested will not need to be present, since most of the propositions can be answered on the basis of your knowledge of its behaviour.

Audio Skills
How often does your cat respond to the sound of food being placed in its dish?

  A Always, as if it had not eaten in days.

  B Sometimes, if it is hungry.

  C Never. You often have to remind it where the food dish *is*.

A loud thunderstorm rolls in during the middle of the night. Your cat would:

  A Act scared as an excuse to sleep in your bed.

  B Be happy just to stay inside for the night, only hopping into your bed if invited to do so.

  C Panic and rave as if the world was about to end.

When you call for your cat using its name, your cat:

  A Perks to attention, but may or may not act on your call.

  B Perks to attention and invariably comes to you.

  C Appears not to recognize its name at all.

Visual Skills
While you're watching TV, your cat likes to:

 A See what else is on by changing the channels.

 B Take the opportunity to jump in your lap.

 C Sit in front of the TV, blocking your view.

Social Skills
When meeting a dog, your cat:

 A Stays well out of the way. Dogs are bigger than cats.

 B Tries to hide.

 C Inspires the dog to think about lunch.

Take out your pet carrier and place it in front of your cat. It will:

 A Run and hide right away.

 B Grudgingly gets in when asked.

 C Jump right in without any prompting.

Domestic Behaviour
Your cat prefers eating:

 A Food from *your* plate.

 B Cat food.

 C Almost anything, especially inedible items such as socks or newspapers.

If your cat wanted to wake you up, it would:

 A Jump directly onto your head or stomach and meow.

 B Meow politely from the foot of the bed.

 C Probably try when you're not at home.

Other scientists offer the theory that cats are very responsive to sudden shifts in the earth's magnetic field, such as those which accompany earthquakes.

The Homing Instinct

Not long ago, Mr Vladimir Dontsov's grey-and-white cat Murka ate the two canaries which shared the Dontsovs' Moscow home with her. As punishment, Murka was banished to Voronezh, 644 km (400 miles) from Moscow. She was there for only two days when she vanished. Much later, she turned up, dirty and hungry, at the Dontsov apartment in Moscow. *Komsomolskaya Pravda*, which related Murka's saga, did not say how long her great trek took her, though it did report that she had lost the tip of her tail and had an injured ear. She was also pregnant. Clearly, it had been an adventurous journey.

Even so, it did not put Murka into the record books, since there are well-authenticated stories of cats making it back home over longer distances.

The cat's well-developed homing instinct has long intrigued scientists. Kittens are born with a very strong instinct towards finding a teat to suck and are usually firmly attached to one within half-an-hour of their birth, having found it with no help from their mother and despite being blind. It is thought that it is their sense of smell that guides them. It is also smell that keeps them attached to their nesting box – their 'homing region'. Older cats also probably follow familiar scents home over short distances. But surely smell cannot account for the way cats can get back home over many miles of unfamiliar territory?

Several series of homing instinct experiments have been carried out on cats by highly respected scientists. Professor Frank Herrick conducted enough simple tests with cats in Cleveland, Ohio, back in the 1920s to come to the conclusion that cats possess a 'directional constant' – a navigational sense that means that a cat does not need to remember the details of its journey away from home to get back to it again.

Later research by German scientists got quite complicated. It involved taking cats away from their homes in covered boxes, so they could not see where they were going, and driving them by tortuous routes to a place some miles away. Here, a maze had been devised based on a central area with passages leading from it to a runway which surrounded the maze and from which six exits led out of the maze. The whole maze was covered so that the cats, once placed in it, could not see sunlight, stars or other possible navigational aids. A significant number of the cats put into the maze chose as their exit one which pointed directly towards home. When the scientists put homing pigeons through the test, they did not do quite so well.

Scientists not convinced that the 'cats-in-the-maze' test was really unflawed in its method, had some of their doubts eased by an American experiment which involved drugging cats with doped food before taking them away from home in a deep sleep. Once fully restored to wakefulness, the cats were tested and most were found to know their way home again.

After all this testing, it is pretty clear that cats do indeed possess some kind of homing mechanism, probably based on a high degree of sensitivity to the earth's geo-magnetic field. This same mechanism is postulated for birds and other animals, including humans. Scientists are not clear yet as to how it works, and are homing in on the iron particles which occur naturally in animal tissue as their best clue to the existence of a built-in biological compass in us all.

The Height Of Perception

Because of the requirements of their highly specialized hunting techniques, cats have much better hearing even than dogs and cer-

tainly than humans. Young, healthy cats can sense the slightest sound and are very good at locating the precise direction it is coming from. They also have a much wider auditory range than humans. Where humans at their best can hear noises up to around 20,000 cycles per second, cats can hear sounds up to a range of over 50,000 cycles per second and perhaps even as high as 100,000 cycles per second in cats in the prime of life.

But a cat also knows its owner's car from others; it can pick out the sound from dozens, even hundreds of other cars that pass the house during the course of a day, and which it ignores.

Experiments show that cats can discriminate finely between musical tones. The French writer Theophile Gautier had a cat who did not care for the sound of a high A, especially when sung. She would sit quietly listening to Gautier accompanying women singers on the piano, reaching out to put a paw over the singer's mouth if she hit that top A. Cats can differentiate between sounds that are only a half-tone different or even, as some series of tests have demonstrated, even one-tenth of a tone . . . it is an ability far beyond the human ear. Thus, it is not too difficult a feat for a cat to pick out the sound of its owner's car.

But if research has made our cat's welcome home explicable in terms of its hearing abilities, it has not done so in terms of that other phenomenon, the cat's obvious awareness that someone close to it is on the way home long before there are any sounds to be heard. And, as another French writer and his cat made clear long ago, it is not just a question of the cat's knowing the time of day and our daily routine.

Alexandre Dumas the Elder lived with his mother and his cat Mysouff in Paris for a long time and acted as a clerk for Louis Philippe, Duc d'Orleans. His office was in the Rue St Honoré, half-an-hour's walk from home. Every morning he went to the office, Mysouff would walk part of the way with him, and when Dumas came back in the afternoon, Mysouff would be back at the spot where they had parted, ready to accompany him on the remainder of his walk home. If by any chance Dumas was delayed at the office or decided to return late, Mysouff would remain comfortably at home, showing no desire to go out even if the door was opened for him. Dumas' mother, in those days before the telephone, was able to use Mysouff as a very reliable guide to the likely time her son would be in for dinner.

Here, something outside the realm of natural science would seem to be at work. That something, according to many writers and researchers in the world of the psyche, is telepathy – the exchange of information between two or more minds by paranormal means. Maurice Howey, writing about cats and telepathy early this century, saw no reason to believe that the faculty of telepathy was not as available to cats as it was to men. He also believed that the exchange of information was a two-way matter: Dumas might have sent a telepathic message to his beloved cat, but cats could also send messages to their owners and Howey cited the writings of Ernest Bozzano to support his contention.

Bozzano recorded that on two occasions, when he was quietly working at his desk, he became possessed by the idea that his cat was in trouble and needed him. On both occasions, lengthy searches for the cat eventually found her in conditions of some danger. Once, she was found in a hedge caught in a rabbit trap, not daring to move lest the slipknot round her neck tightened, and on the other occasion she was found trapped in an empty attic room. On the second incident Bozzano wrote that he eventually found his cat because a clear picture – a sort of mental photograph – suddenly came into his mind of the small, little-used room in which he found the cat.

Since Howey's day, scientists researching in the field of parapsychology have investigated apparent 'telepathic' relationships between cats and their owners in an attempt to understand how cats are able to find their owners by travelling long distances over unfamiliar territory.

We saw a few pages back how a cat's homing instinct – the desire to get back to home territory from somewhere unfamiliar and far off – may be accounted for in scientific terms. But the cat's other homing instinct, in which the desire to return to the company of its owner, or former owner, is very much stronger than the desire to stay in its familiar territory, is still virtually inexplicable except in terms of some form of extra-sensory perception.

Just how do you explain scientifically the journeys of cats like two-year-old Pooh who, in 1974, walked 200 miles from Georgia to South Carolina in the USA to find the owners who had left him behind when they had moved house? The journey took him four months and involved constant, determined travelling across unknown territory towards a goal he had never seen, but knew existed.

Dr Joseph Rhine who, with other scientists at Duke University's Parapsychology Laboratory, appraised hundreds of accounts of animals who had apparently been able to find lost companions over long distances on unfamiliar country, came to the conclusion that some animals were certainly capable of this feat, but came to no firm scientific conclusions.

Perhaps one can leave the final word to Maurice Howey: 'The gulf which usually separates man from his less-evolved brother is not unbridgeable, and that the law underlying the mysterious faculty of Telepathy, is the union of the many in the One. A single heart beats through all the manifestations of Life. And vibrant chords attuned in sympathy unite all sentient beings, so that communication is always possible between those who love.'

Safe Landings

New York City with its high-rise apartment buildings is a dangerous place for cats. In one five-month period 132 cats were taken to the city's animal medical centre suffering from 'high rise syndrome' – a complex array of fractures and other injuries received by falling from a great height.

Most of the cats had fallen more than two storeys and had landed on concrete. One cat had fallen 32 storeys – nearly 152 m (500 ft); it was sent home 48 hours after it was admitted, having suffered a chipped tooth and minor thoracic injuries. A human being would have been killed.

Two vets at the animal medical centre, Dr Wayne Witney and Dr Cheryl Mehlhaff, made a study of the 132 cats and found that 90 per cent of those they treated survived to tell the tale, and of those that did not, most were put down at their owners' request, sometimes because the owner could not afford to pay the veterinary fees. Surprisingly, the vets also found that the greater the fall, the better the chance of survival: 22 of the cats fell more than seven storeys and only one of them died of the fall.

How do cats do it? According to Witney and Mehlhaff, it is all a mixture of physics, anatomy and evolution.

For a start, cats have a much larger surface area in relation to their volume than humans: thus, their maximum rate of descent is lower and is reached more quickly, and the stresses caused by impact are much less.

Even so, cats generally suffer less severe injuries from falling than do dogs, so something else is involved. Which is where genetics and anatomy come in.

Cats are believed to have descended from animals which lived in trees and have inherited the safety mechanisms which allowed survival in such an environment. They also have good stereoscopic vision. When a cat falls from a height, an acutely refined gyro-scopic reflex – a legacy of its arborial ancestry – comes into play, the cat twists round in mid-air and lands on all four paws. Once the cat reaches terminal velocity in mid-air, its muscles relax so that its legs splay out horizontally, allowing it to come down parachute-fashion, rather like a flying squirrel. This maximizes the surface area and the air-braking, so that the effects of impact on any one part of the body are minimal.

So, when the Humane Society of America dubbed cats 'the genetically engineered pet for working people', they could have added, 'especially if they live in tall buildings'.

Survival Tactics

A shipping company cat from Dartford in Kent, England, inadver-tently emigrated to Australia in 1990. The female black puss was accidentally crated up in a container with a Mercedes-Benz car being shipped from Britain to Adelaide, South Australia, and sur-vived a 48-day journey without food or water, apart from conden-sation in the container.

She caused quite a stir when she arrived in Adelaide, where she was taken into custody by South Australian Department of Agri-culture quarantine officials. They christened her Mercedes and started a publicity campaign to get the $A1620-worth of quaran-tine costs paid so that they could eventually let her out of their custody.

For a while, it looked as if Mercedes would set an Australian all-comers' record for the most expensive feline to be adopted in the country. But she did not have to spend the statutory nine months in quarantine because officials were able to verify that back in Britain she had been a properly cared-for pet, with little chance of having come into contact with rabies. So they threw a party with champagne and orange juice for the human guests and special titbits for Mercedes, before releasing her into the care of her new owner, Mrs Mila Skartvedt, the owner of the Mercedes-Benz with which the cat had hitched its ride Down Under.

As for the 'substantial leftovers' from the fund set up to pay Mercedes' quarantine expenses, they were distributed among cat care groups in Adelaide and everyone was happy.

Mercedes' 48 days of living on condensation in her container did not set a distance record. This is held by a cat called Felix who flew 289.674 km (180,000 miles) in the hold of a jumbo jet in 1987 before he was caught 29 days after he climbed out of his travelling box. Like Mercedes, Felix survived by licking condensation.

The reason both cats survived so long without food or reasonable amounts of water is that cats are able to retain fluid in their bodies to a much greater extent than humans. They also know instinctively to remain as inactive as possible, keeping the body temperature low to slow down the rate of fluid loss.

Ball Skills

Cats have their own ideas about playing with balls. Sometimes they are irresistibly attracted to them, at other times they will allow a ball to pass under their noses without twitching a whisker.

There is an often-repeated story of a cat who used to perform at the Folies Bergère in Paris. For one audience the cat would perform beautifully, doing the things for which it had been trained, including jumping through hoops and sitting nonchalantly on top of a large rubber ball, with grace and style; for another audience, the cat might produce bits of its show, then ignore the rest of the proceedings; for yet another audience the cat might appear to be simply part of the scenery, so small would be its contribution to what was happening on stage. Mood was all.

Mark Twain's kitten, Tammany, on the other hand, liked hitting balls about. She used to curl up in a corner pocket of Twain's pool table and swipe out with her paw to redirect balls headed towards the opposite corner pocket. Twain had to introduce a house rule to the game which called for the ball to be retrieved and put back as closely as possible on its original spot so that the shot could be taken again.

Thomas the cat, who lived at a house 180 m (200 yards) from the 15th green of the Weston-super-Mare golf club in Avon, England, just liked balls. In one year, he stole 500 golf balls from the green and carried them home. Since there must have been several hundred angry golfers not far away, it took a brave owner to confess to Thomas's crime.

One can't help wondering what Thomas wanted with all those balls. Perhaps he just liked to see them all hoarded together in an interesting heap. Maybe he thought they were eggs and he could incubate them. Silly idea? Not as silly as one might think. In her book *The Cat's Whiskers*, actress and catperson Beryl Reid tells how her charming and handsome tabby, Patrick, tended two clutches of eggs laid by Beryl's Muscovy duck, Jemima. Patrick would sit on the eggs while Jemima was in the river washing her feathers and he never broke one. Unfortunately, neither clutch came to anything and Jemima smashed the eggs, so no one ever knew if Patrick would have turned out to be a good stepfather to a group of ducklings.

End Of The Line . . . Almost!

Sometimes, when the chips are down, even a cat's great skills, physical endowments and mental abilities are not enough to save him from trouble and he needs help from people. Here are two stories of cats being rescued from certain death by brave men.

The first story proves that mouth-to-mouth resuscitation does work on cats. In July 1977, newspapers reported that a deeply unconscious cat was brought out of a burning cottage in Stroud, Gloucestershire. The fire brigade chief at the scene used mouth-to-mouth resuscitation on the cat for 20 minutes, believing that since the cat had not been burnt, but overcome by smoke, it could be revived. He was right. The cat survived to live out a few more of its nine lives.

The great adventure of Sammy, a long-haired ginger-and-white cat, took place in Manchester at Christmastime. Sammy, trying to escape from a pack of dogs on his trail, shot up the metal ladder of a 45 m (150 ft) brick chimney in a mill yard. He settled on a double rung for the night, the rain pelting down on him and turning to ice crystals as the long hours to daylight wore on.

In the morning, Sammy was spotted by workers at the mill, who, by chance, included Mr Fred Dibnah, a steeplejack who had achieved some fame by being filmed at work by BBC Television. Soon, news television cameras were on the scene to film Sammy's plight. Armed with a wire mesh basket to bring Sammy down and some sardines to entice him into the basket, Mr Dibnah went up the ladder after the cat in driving rain and fierce wind.

Sammy retreated right to the top of the chimney and refused to be enticed by the sardines. Eventually, Mr Dibnah climbed back down again and Sammy had to spend another long night at the top of the chimney, with only his fur to insulate him against the appalling weather conditions.

Next day, Mr Dibnah had another attempt at rescuing Sammy, but by now the cat was frozen and would not budge. By now, too, he was front-page news in most of the national newspapers, some of which had christened him 'Lofty'.

Down below, Gerry Rogers, a worker from a nearby rubber factory, had been following events in the mill yard closely. In his lunch break he went to the yard to have a look at poor Sammy. Suddenly, still wearing his workplace green wellies, he started up the metal ladder on the chimney's side. Thirty minutes later, he had managed to grab Sammy and brought him down 30 m (100 ft) with considerable difficulty. At this point, Mr Dibnah was able to hoist the wire basket up to Gerry, who stuffed Sammy into it and brought him down to the ground. The cheers from the waiting crowd of workers, newspaper reporters and television cameramen echoed round the mill yard.

My hero!